Key to Map Numbers

1 **110A Piccadilly** — *apartment of Lord Peter Wimsey*

2 **New Scotland Yard** — *police headquarters*

3 **12 A Great Ormond Street** — *apartment of Detective-Inspector Charles Parker*

4 **The Old Bailey** — *court where Harriet Vane was tried*

5 **Simpsons** — *men's restaurant where Lord Peter took Pamela Dean*

6 **Mecklenburg Square** — *Harriet Vane's apartment (also Dorothy Sayers')*

7 **Great James Street** — *Dorothy Sayers' first apartment*

8 **Benson's (on Kingsway) and Pym's Publicity (on Southampton Row)**

9 **West End** — *the London theater district, bounded by Oxford Street, Green Park, the Thames River, and Aldwich; center is Piccadilly Circus*

10 **Soho district** — *foreign restaurant area*

11 **St. Thomas' Regent's Street Church** — *where Emperor Constantine was performed*

12 **St. Anne's Soho Church** — *where Dorothy Sayers' ashes are buried*

13 **St. Margaret's Westminster Church** — *where Dorothy Sayers' memorial service was held*

14 **28 St. John's Wood Terrace** — *where Marjorie Barber and Muriel St. Clare Byrne lived*

15 **Mayfair district** — *society's home — where the duke of Denver lives*

16 **No. 2 South Audley Square** — *where Harriet and Lord Peter live; really the University Women's Club*

17 **The Detection Club** — *where Dorothy presided as the Ruler; also site of the Soviet Club*

18 **Fleet Street** — *home of London's newspapers*

19 **Bloomsbury district** — *intellectual Bohemia*

20 **Chelsea district** — *artists' area*

21 **Battersea district** — *where Whose Body? takes place*

22 **British Museum** — *haunt of scholars and sleuths*

23 **Bayswater district** — *where The Documents in the Case takes place*

24 **Somerset House** — *national registry of births*

25 **97A St. George's Square** — *The Cattery, home of Miss Climpson*

26 **Staple Inn** — *Mr. Murbles' law office*

Dorothy L. Sayers'
London:
Fact and Fiction

MAKER AND CRAFTSMAN

The Story of Dorothy L. Sayers

MAKER AND CRAFTSMAN

The Story of Dorothy L. Sayers

by

Alzina Stone Dale

WILLIAM B. EERDMANS PUBLISHING COMPANY

GRAND RAPIDS, MICHIGAN

Library of Congress Cataloging in Publication Data

Dale, Alzina Stone, 1931–
   Maker and craftsman.

   SUMMARY: Recounts the life of the English author who
created the urbane, aristocratic sleuth, Lord Peter
Wimsey.
   1. Sayers, Dorothy Leigh, 1893–1957—Biography.
2. Authors, English—20th century—Biography.
[1. Sayers, Dorothy Leigh, 1893–1957. 2. Authors,
English] I. Title.
PR6037.A95Z63 823'.9'12 [92] 78-15640
ISBN 0-8028-3515-5

TO
That Communion of Saints,
My Family and Friends,
Through Whose Faith This Book was Born

ACKNOWLEDGMENTS

Through A. Watkins, Inc. and David Higham Ltd. permission to quote from the works of Dorothy L. Sayers has been granted by Mr. A. Fleming and the Sayers estate as follows:

HARPER & ROW and VICTOR GOLLANCZ:

Busman's Honeymoon (New York: Harcourt Brace, 1937; Harpers, 1960) (London: Victor Gollancz, 1937), copyright by Dorothy L. Sayers, 1937.

Gaudy Night (New York: Harcourt Brace, 1936; Harpers, 1960) (London: Victor Gollancz, 1935), copyright by Dorothy L. Sayers, 1935.

Unnatural Death (New York: The Dial Press, 1928; Harcourt Brace, 1938; Harpers, 1955) (London: E. Benn, 1927; Victor Gollancz, 1935), copyright by Dorothy L. Sayers, 1927.

The Unpleasantness at the Bellona Club (New York: Payson & Clarke, 1928; Harpers, 1956) (London: E. Benn, 1927; Victor Gollancz, 1935), copyright by Dorothy L. Sayers, 1928.

Murder Must Advertise (New York: Harcourt Brace, 1933; Harpers, 1959) (London: Victor Gollancz, 1933), copyright by Dorothy L. Sayers, 1933.

Whose Body? (New York: Brewer & Warren, 1930; Harcourt Brace, 1936; Harpers, 1958) (London: Victor Gollancz, 1930), copyright by Dorothy L. Sayers, 1930.

Five Red Herrings (New York: Brewer, Warren & Putnam, 1931; Harpers, 1958) (London: Victor Gollancz, 1931), copyright by Dorothy L. Sayers, 1931.

The Man Born to Be King (New York: Harpers, 1943; Grand Rapids: William B. Eerdmans, 1970) (London: Victor Gollancz, 1943), copyright by Dorothy L. Sayers, 1943.

The Dorothy L. Sayers Literary and Historical Society, Witham, England, permission to quote from the Society's Newsletters and Proceedings to which they hold the copyright, 1975 to date. All materials quoted therein which are by Dorothy L. Sayers are copyright © by Anthony Fleming, 1978.

Dr. Barbara Reynolds, permission to use materials from her taped lectures at Wheaton College 1975–78, copyright by Barbara Reynolds, 1978.

Somerville College, permission to quote from the Dorothy L. Sayers Memorial Tablet in Somerville Chapel, as well as permission to use the drawings in *Somerville College.*

John Gilroy, R. A., permission to use his drawings of Dorothy L. Sayers.

Wilfred Scott-Giles, OBE, permission to use his drawings of the Wimsey Arms, copyright Wilfred Scott-Giles, 1977.

This book could never have been written without the aid and comfort of the Dorothy L. Sayers Literary and Historical Society, Roslyn House, Witham, England, and the Wade Collection at Wheaton College, Wheaton, Illinois, where everyone has been unfailingly kind and helpful. I also owe a great debt of thanks to Dorothy L. Sayers' friends, particularly to Dr. Barbara Reynolds, Muriel St. Clare Byrne, Wilfred Scott-Giles, John Gilroy, Dorothy Rowe, and Charis U. Frankenburg and her publisher, Galaxy Books, for the material they have given me. I want to thank all those who patiently answered my questions: James Brabazon, Joe R. Christopher, Colleen Gilbert, E. R. Gregory, Alice Hadfield, Margaret Hannay, Fr. Walter Hooper, Christe McMenomy, Dr. Michael Ramsey, Catharine Seybold, Ann Schreurs, Dr. Carroll Simcox, Rosamund Sprague, the librarian of Lambeth Palace, and the historiographer of the See of Chichester. Earlier accounts of Miss Sayers' life by Vera Brittain, Carolyn Heilbrun, Janet Hitchman, Roderick Jellema, Ralph Hone, and James Sandoe helped to make mine possible, while I could not have worked without the checklists and chronologies of Joe R. Christopher and Margaret Burger and Robert Harmon. I want to thank both Barbara Craig and the librarian, Pauline Adams, at Somerville College, not only for permission to quote from the Sayers Memorial tablet in the chapel, but also for the time and effort which went into tracking down pictures of Somerville College and for arranging that permission be granted to use the drawings from Muriel St. Clare Byrne and Catherine Hope Mansfield's *Somerville College.* Most of all I want to thank Anthony Fleming for permission to quote from Miss Sayers' own works, both published and unpublished.

Finally, to follow in the footsteps of my favorite subject, I must thank both Dorothy Sharpless Strang and Mary McDermott Shideler for the "extreme of womanly patience with which they read and reread the tale of Dorothy L. Sayers as it was being written." The mistakes in it, of course, are my own.

CONTENTS

A Word to the Reader   xiii

1. Oxford and the Fens   1
2. The Pert Poll-Parrot in Looking Glass Land   9
3. The Poet   20
4. Alma Mater   31
5. Domina   50
6. Advertising and the Aristocracy   63
7. Private Lives   72
8. Success   80
9. Religious Dramatist   101
10. Masterpiece   113
11. Translator of Dante   130
12. Last Works   145
    Postscript   155

A WORD TO THE READER

DOROTHY LEIGH SAYERS WAS AN ENERGETIC AND enthusiastic person at home in many worlds. She liked riding a motorcycle, making up crossword puzzles, and writing plays about the New Testament. She had a miraculous gift for languages and a fantastic sense of humor. She wrote chatty, amusing letters to her friends, while she also gave lectures on intellectual subjects that were both clear and entertaining. Reading them today makes her seem to be here in person—a big, impressive woman, her spectacles perched on her nose before her blue, nearsighted eyes, her short gray hair shoved back in the mannish style of the 1920s, talking with you in her deep, attractive voice and making occasional, emphatic gestures with her beautiful hands.

Many of her readers cannot imagine how one person could be a successful detective story writer, a creator of religious plays, and a translator of the medieval poet Dante. What these people miss when they try to pigeonhole Dorothy in one category or another is the fact that her sly sense of humor, her ability to explain the ideas of one generation to another, and her Christian beliefs appear in everything she wrote. By not reading all her work, they miss knowing all about Dorothy herself, who in many ways was her own best character.

Dorothy claimed that her own life was not sensational enough for the headline writers of *The Local Gossip*. But like most writers, she often used people and places she knew as a starting place. Then she mischievously claimed that her books all took place in a "Cloud-Cuckooland" where nobody lives.

She was a very private person who felt that what she had to say she said in her writing. She did not live her personal life to make "good copy" for publicity, but she did have strong opinions and was never afraid to express them. Like other authors who have given birth to a famous character, she found her detective hero Lord Peter Wimsey forever following her like Mary's little lamb. Even so, she moved into other literary fields successfully, returning to her earliest interests, and taking her public with her.

It has been said that the older Dorothy grew and the more she wrote about God and his creation, the more religious she became. The truth is both simpler and harder to understand. As she wrote, all her talents and interests came together to make her real calling clear to her. Her skill in languages, her ability as a storyteller, her talent as a popularizer of difficult ideas, and her Christian convictions, all came together in her work on the life of Christ and her translation of Dante. She had always thought that man is like God in his ability to create, and to her, creation is another name for work.

Critics have said that because Dorothy was "only" a mystery writer, she had no business being rude if interrupted, bored by fools, amusing herself at the public's expense, hiding her private life, falling in love, or getting fat. No wonder Dorothy thought that biographies are highly overrated. This book is neither the first nor the last book to be written about Dorothy L. Sayers. It hopes to be as fair, accurate, and amusing as she was herself and to help you enjoy the joke she liked to tell about the schoolboy who wrote,

"And then there was Miss Dorothy Sayers who turned from a life of crime to join the Church of England."

A.D.

1

OXFORD AND THE FENS

DOROTHY LEIGH SAYERS WAS BORN AT OXFORD ON JUNE 13, 1893, four years before Queen Victoria's Diamond Jubilee, when it seemed as if the sun would never set upon the vast British Empire. She was the only child of the Reverend Henry Sayers and his wife, Helen Mary. On July 15 she was baptized in Christ Church Cathedral by her father with the names "Dorothy," which means "gift of God" in Greek, and "Leigh," which was Mrs. Sayers' maiden name.

Her father was headmaster of the University Cathedral Choir School which was part of Christ Church College. After graduating from Oxford in 1879, he had been ordained a minister in the Church of England. His first job had been as chaplain at Christ Church College, then at New College, Oxford. Next he was a schoolmaster, and finally headmaster, at St. Michael's College, Tenbury, and later at the Cathedral School at Hereford. Mr. Sayers was not only a good musician, but also a classics scholar. Among other duties he taught Latin to the small choirboys of his school, who sang at the university services.

On her mother's side Dorothy was related to a famous writer. Mrs. Sayers' father was a solicitor, or family lawyer, but she was also the grand-niece of Percival Leigh, who had been one of the original staff of *Punch*. This famous British magazine was named for the puppet "Punch" of the Punch and Judy shows, and it is still full of clever cartoons and comments on the world.

Dorothy's great-uncle was known as the "Professor" because he wrote articles in a mock-intellectual style full of clever parodies and puns on famous literature. He was a very careful writer who took great pains with his work. There were many stories about Mr. Leigh, who was known as a bit eccentric. He wore old clothes in public and marched down busy London streets reciting Shakespeare at the top of his lungs. All her life Dorothy took great pride in the name "Leigh" and got very angry if people left out her middle initial. Quite young, she decided to be a writer, too.

When Dorothy was born, Oxford was a sleepy little market town which was also the home of England's oldest university. The railroad had not been allowed to run through the center of town, and none of its old, medieval buildings had been torn down to widen its winding, narrow streets. Only the main avenues like the High were paved with stone, and there were no automobiles. Seen from its surrounding hills, Oxford was a beautiful little medieval city, all tall spires and gray gothic towers.

The university was made up of independent colleges where the students lived and ate. A student belonged to his college, but he was "up" at Oxford. Most of the colleges were built many centuries ago. They each had two or three quadrangles, or groups of buildings joined together to form a central courtyard. Each college had its own chapel, library, and dining hall, and a walled garden for the dons, or professors and tutors, to walk in. The college was entered only by a narrow gateway from the street outside.

Christ Church College, where Dorothy's father was headmaster of the Choir School, was begun by Cardinal Wolsey in 1524. He was the chief minister of King Henry VIII until he fell from power for opposing the king's divorce.

The college's Tom Quad is the biggest quadrangle at Oxford. It has a stone cloister, or covered passageway, along its inner walls which looks out on a lush, wide lawn. In the center of the lawn is a shallow stone fountain called "Mercury," where giant goldfish swim and snap at breadcrumbs.

Above its main gatehouse rises the Tom Tower, which houses the great Tom bell. At 9:05 every evening, the Sayers household at No. I Brewer Street would hear Great Tom tolling 101 strokes in honor of the one hundred and one original members of Christ Church College. The bell was warning all Oxford undergraduates that they must be inside their colleges. The sound of bells was among Dorothy's earliest memories. "Each after each, from all the towers of Oxford, clocks struck... in a tumbling cascade of friendly disagreement."

Dorothy's father was interested in church architecture and antiquities, which is the study of ancient historical sites and objects, and he passed his enthusiasm on to Dorothy. She said that everyone is either "gothic" or "classical" by instinct, and her choice always was the tall, branching lines of medieval buildings rather than square, boxlike classic temples.

During her own lifetime Oxford changed greatly, becoming a much larger and dirtier city famous for manufacturing automobiles. But nothing ever erased Dorothy's first vision of Oxford as an eternal city, sacred to the world of ideas. "It might be an old-fashioned city, with inconvenient buildings and narrow streets... but her foundations were set upon the holy hills and her spires touched heaven."

Oxford was the home of many famous men. One of the best known was the shy, retired professor of mathematics who had written *Alice in Wonderland* under the pen name Lewis Carroll. Dorothy's nurse told her that when the elderly don with the mane of wavy gray hair met them walking, he always smiled at her in her buggy. Lewis Carroll had written *Alice* for Alice Liddell, the daughter of the head of Christ Church College, and her wonderful adventures all began on the river near the Christ Church meadows. When Dorothy read *Alice* and its sequel, *Through the Looking Glass*, which takes place on a giant chessboard, she could imagine that she was the little girl who chased the White Rabbit down the hole. She knew the magical, topsy-turvy world of Lewis Carroll, as well as other children's classics from Mother Goose to Rudyard Kipling, backwards and forwards, and the characters she later created herself often quote from them.

When Dorothy was four and a half her father was offered the job of parish priest in a Fens parish. The Fens are low flatlands in the east of England near the North Sea. Originally most of the land was swampy, but in about the 17th century it was drained for farming. The parish he was offered was called Bluntisham-cun-Earith. Earith was one of the ancient "ports," or bridges, over the marshes to the Isle of Ely with its beautiful gothic cathedral built on high land that had been fortified and defended since Roman times. Ely is not now a true island, but it is still a safe, high place above the floods.

The salary Mr. Sayers was offered was a good one for the time—over fifteen hundred pounds a year, or about seven thousand dollars. It was more than he was paid for running the university Choir School, and like many people then, he was supporting other members of his family as well as his own wife and child. The idea of moving to the bleak, isolated Fens, where the strong winds from the sea blew yearlong, was not appealing after cozy, civilized Oxford, but living would be cheaper, and the Sayers' small medieval townhouse on Brewer Street next door to the new Cathedral School was crowded. Living with the Sayers were Mrs. Sayers' sister, Aunt Maud, with her parrot, Grandmother Sayers, Dorothy's nurse, and other servants. The Sayers decided that a big old country rectory would be better, so in 1897 the family said good-bye to Oxford.

Dorothy clearly remembered her own arrival in January

at Bluntisham Rectory. She was escorted by her nurse and by her aunt Maud, called Aunt Leigh, with her parrot in his covered cage. Dorothy was all dressed up in a brown pelisse, or cloak trimmed with fur, and wore a bonnet with matching feathers. The weather had been mild that winter and on the lawn bright yellow monksbane was already blooming. Her father told her the legend that monksbane grew only where the ground had been "watered" with Roman blood in some ancient battle, and showed her the remains of a Roman camp nearby.

The countryside about Bluntisham was full of romantic tales out of history—about Boadicea, the Briton Queen who defied the Roman legions, or outlaws like Hereward the Wake, who held off William the Norman Conqueror. The local villagers told her stories about them as if they were ghosts and bogeymen who haunted the swamps, and Dorothy early developed a feeling for the reality of the past and its relationship with the present. Although many of the great Fens abbeys were in ruins, there were still many tall, handsome gothic churches left for Mr. Sayers to show Dorothy, passing on his enthusiasm for architecture, which led her in turn to call God "the Master Builder."

In Oxford the Sayers family had had modern gas lights and running water. But in Bluntisham Rectory they used oil lamps which a maid brought in at dusk and set in wall brackets. There were candles in holders for each person to take when he went upstairs to bed. The plumbing was also very primitive and the heating done mostly with fireplaces, so that the rectory could be very chilly.

As a small child Dorothy grew used to the Fens' winter floods. Year after year someone would say at breakfast, "We've been having a lot of rain; they'll be letting the 'water out.'"

From the front windows of the rectory at Bluntisham she would see the river overflow, turning fields and pastures into sheets of standing water. Then she and her nurse bundled up to walk to the Seven-Holes Bridge or the Hermitage Sluice, or floodgate, at Earith, to watch the water come swirling through the opened gates into the river, sparing as much farmland as possible.

In the middle ages the bishop of Ely, who controlled the whole area where Dorothy now lived, had established a keeper who lived alone at a hermitage and mended the bridges and floodgates when they needed repair. During floods, he also ran the local ferry. When Dorothy was young, her father's parishioners would often be late to church if they lived in the outlying houses, because they had to wait for the ferry. On train trips looking out the window she saw what seemed the whole world covered by water, with broken lines where the hedges were and only the large tops of the willow and poplar trees showing. Once, the river froze solid, and people skated all the way from Earith to Ely.

Dorothy also grew used to roads that ran straight mile after mile, past windmills and farmhouses and rows of umbrella-like elms and drainage dykes. Here and there tall, impressive Fen churches looked down on clusters of red-roofed houses surrounded by windswept fields of sheep grazing below the sky. Often she had to cross a bridge to reach a house. Some towns had been stranded inland by the receding seas and had old warehouses and piers where ships once docked.

Normally, when parts of the Fens are "drowned" every year, no great damage is done. But as Dorothy realized when she had grown up, there was something more deadly about the slow attack of the cold North Sea against the Fen country than about the more dramatic breakers of the Atlantic Ocean that pound the rocky southern coast. Over the centuries the Fens' silent tides had redrawn the map, devoured whole towns, and lain in wait to reclaim the drained land. In the Fens the parish church and the rectory were often built a short distance away from the village itself on higher ground. Even today if the drains and dykes crumble, the Fenland churches with their lofty bell towers built to give warning are places where people can flee to safety.

Life in the Fens was lonely, and the minister was often the main link with the outside world. In several of her novels Dorothy describes with affection the daily life of a rural parish priest, which she knew firsthand. Most of the clergymen in her stories have a quiet, unworldly authority in their dealings with people. They are kind and available in trouble, but they are also absent-minded and a bit childlike at times. Their wives often have to look out for them in practical matters.

The Sayers rectory was a large stone mansion. It had a central, squarish Georgian facade with a pillared porch and two wings hung with ivy. Tall chimneys with chimney pots rose from its high, flat roof. It looked more like a hotel than a private house, and Dorothy liked to tell about the time that a visitor got lost. He had passed by the rectory, but assumed that any place that big could not be the Sayers home. He explained that he had thought it must be a gentleman's house, to which Dorothy's father had retorted, "We hope it is!"

In front of the rectory facing the road was a long, sloping lawn surrounded by big old trees. About two miles beyond the lawn's iron fence lay the open Fens. In back of the house was another lawn, a small wood, and a walled kitchen garden.

A picture of Dorothy at this age shows her to have been a round-faced, chubby child with thick black hair, bobbed about her ears Christopher Robin style. Her blue eyes are faintly shut against the glare, but her wide mouth is just about to smile. She is wearing a beautiful Van Dyke lace collar over her best dress, but she looks like a cheerful little tomboy, ruler of her own small world and much amused by it. It is easy to see why her father jokingly called her "little humbug" when she came down in her nightgown to say goodnight, interrupting a tutoring session with a local girl.

Dorothy's character Harriet Vane grew up in the country, too. Harriet's father was the village doctor instead of the village minister, but from the standpoint of social class and income, they were much alike. And like little Miss Vane, little Miss Sayers also rode beside her father in the pony trap, pretending to drive, and stopped to visit parishioners, who would feed her treats like strawberries and seedcake.

"In London," Dorothy once said, "anybody, at any moment, might do or become anything. But in a village, they were all . . . themselves; parson, organist, sweep, duke's son and doctor's daughter, moving like chessmen upon their allotted squares."

2

THE PERT POLL-PARROT
IN LOOKING
GLASS LAND

IN DESCRIBING HER OWN EARLY EDUCATION DOROTHY told about the kind of child she had been.

"Looking back on myself, since I am the child I know best and the only child I can pretend to know from inside, I recognize three stages of development. These, in a rough-and-ready fashion, I will call the Poll-Parrot, the Pert, and the Poetic."

From about nine years to eleven, she was the poll-parrot, who liked to memorize lists and jibberish like advertising jingles. From twelve to fourteen she was pert, fond of contradicting her elders. In the poetic period from fifteen on, she was a moody and preoccupied adolescent.

When Dorothy was growing up, most middle-class fathers did not educate their daughters the way they did their sons. The boys were usually sent away to school as early as seven or eight. They went first to a "prep," or preparatory school, to learn Latin, Greek, and mathematics, so that they could pass the examinations for high school. When the boys were about twelve they went to high school, where they were taught to pass the even stiffer examinations for the universities like Oxford or Cambridge. The famous English "public schools," such as Eton or Harrow, are private boarding schools for boys which are open to anyone who can pass their examinations and pay the tuition.

Girls, however, usually stayed at home and were taught languages like French or German, drawing, music, and social manners—first by their mothers or nurses and then by a governess—until they were considered old enough to have a debut. Beatrice Potter, who wrote *Peter Rabbit,* had a governess until she was sixteen. Her parents did not approve of her writing books, and they did not let her leave home until she was nearly forty. Virginia Woolf, a famous novelist and contemporary of Dorothy's, was the daughter of Sir Leslie Stephen, who wrote books on literature. But she had to educate herself by reading her father's library, while her brothers were all sent to Cambridge.

On the other hand, a few more progressive families, particularly those who were themselves in education, thought that girls had just as much right to higher education as did boys. Some of them sent their daughters to girls' boarding schools when they were twelve or thirteen, or sent them to the good day schools in cities like Oxford or London. Dorothy's Oxford friend Charis Barnett went to London's famous St. Paul's School for Girls.

Except for some brilliant boys who won scholarships, the general public did not get much schooling at all. Although there were Church-run schools and other private schools, there was no compulsory education in England before 1870, and it was only in 1902 that the state began to support any public high schools. Most children learned a little reading, writing, and arithmetic, and then got jobs in shops or factories or as servants.

Although her own family were not well known, Dorothy grew up in a home which was like the ones that produced several generations of brilliant thinkers and doers in English life. The Darwins and Huxleys, who were scientists, or the

Arnolds and Macaulays, who ran schools and were professors and ministers, were all interested in learning for its own sake. They filled their homes and their children's lives with books and ideas.

These families were also interested in the fight to win women the right to vote, to have an education like a man's, to hold office, and to have careers. Their children, both boys and girls, learned to talk and think by listening to their parents and their friends. They were not raised only by servants, and they had freer childhoods, with less supervision than customary. Dorothy had the run of the rectory, and her parents always talked to her as they would to an adult.

When Dorothy arrived at Bluntisham in 1897, she could already read. She could not remember when she learned how. Then, when she was not quite seven, her father decided to teach her Latin. She said she was never sure if he missed the small choir boys from his school in Oxford, or if he was concerned about her education. But it seems likely that Mr. Sayers realized very early that Dorothy was extremely bright and planned for her to have a university education.

One morning her father appeared in the nursery carrying a shabby black book, and said to her, "I think, my dear, that you are now old enough to begin to learn Latin."

Dorothy was very pleased by the idea. As an only child in a houseful of adults, she was used to being the center of attention, and she enjoyed it. She felt that learning Latin would make her superior to her mother, Aunt Leigh, and her nurse. But she also knew that she would have to work to catch up with her grandmother, because old Mrs. Sayers had been well educated for her day. She knew some Latin, read Italian, and owned many books, which Dorothy later inherited.

Mr. Sayers sat down in the old nursery chair by the fire, put his arm about Dorothy so she wouldn't wriggle, and opened his book. It was a standard Latin grammar. He read aloud the mysterious Latin formula for declining a noun of the first declension:

> *mensa*: a table
> *mensa*: O table!
> *mensam*: a table
> *mensae*: of a table
> *mensae*: to a table
> *mensa*: by, with, or from a table.

Then he explained to Dorothy that the ancient Romans, the same people who had built the fort nearby, had the odd habit of changing the endings of their nouns. Dorothy accepted this fact calmly because life was full of odd things. A dog had only four feet, but a beetle had six. She did wonder why anybody would ever want to shout, "O table!"

That first morning she and her father got to the romantic situation in which the "poeta puellae rosas dat" (the poet gives roses to the girl). She thought it was very funny that the Latin words for poet, sailor, and farmer all end in "a" like a girl's name. When they had finished the first exercise, Mr. Sayers left, leaving her the book so that she could memorize the declension for *mensa*. Dorothy quickly did so and then ran downstairs to show off her new learning in the kitchen.

Their Latin lesson became a daily event. Once Dorothy knew enough Latin, she and her father marched with Caesar's army, built Roman walls with Balbo, and admired the conduct of Cornelia, the Roman matron who brought up her children to be good citizens. Although her father was not an exciting teacher, those early years were fun, and at that time she liked Latin better than French, which she was also beginning to learn.

The big, drafty, inconvenient rectory did at least have room for the whole family to go about their affairs independently. Grandmother Sayers and Aunt Leigh both had maids and private sitting rooms, while Dorothy's busy mother had what she called her "den." Mr. Sayers had a large study where he tutored local boys and girls and prepared his sermons. He used to stride up and down reciting his sermons aloud as he wrote them. Dorothy and her nurse occupied the nursery rooms on the top floor, where English children usually were kept out of sight and sound of the adults much of the time.

Her day nursery had a fireplace with a high screen and window guards to keep small children from falling out. In the room were a table and chairs and some maps and plenty of books. On the night nursery walls was a frieze of horses all around the room that Dorothy loved and remembered. Her nurse slept up there with her, and even if there had been several children in the Sayers family, or when her cousins came to visit, they would all sleep together in these nursery rooms. No child was given a private room or much privacy until he or she was considered grown up.

Dorothy's first lesson in reading, writing, and arithmetic were given to her by her nurse with help from her mother and aunt. In an amusing little book called *Even the Parrot*, which Dorothy wrote during the Second World War, the main characters are a very bossy nurse called Nanna and two very pert children who contradict her all the time. But Nanna gets the last word because her word is law in the nursery.

When Dorothy appeared in the drawing room or dining room, she was expected to be seen and not heard. She must not speak unless she was spoken to, and like most children in those days, she spent a good deal of time in the kitchen with the Sayers servants. Although they lived so far out in the country that servants were hard to keep, they had several maids, Dorothy's nurse, the cook, a daily cleaning woman, a gardener, and a stable boy. These servants had their own social life in what was known as the "servants' hall."

Here Dorothy heard local and some national gossip. Her father read papers like *The Times* and *The Spectator*, but his servants read the shorter, simpler, more sensational newspapers which took the place of television today. Public events of her childhood, like old Queen Victoria's Diamond Jubilee in 1897, or her funeral with four kings riding in the cortege in January 1901, were discussed not only in the dining room but in the kitchen. Dorothy probably wore a black armband in mourning for the queen and made flags or banners to decorate the rectory for the coronation of Victoria's son, King Edward VII. She went to local celebrations in his honor, because very few people would travel all the way to London to see the official parade. When the Boer War broke out in South Africa in 1899, the servants and local villagers were much concerned, for it was their sons and husbands who were leaving for the army. The great excitement when the town of Mafeking was saved and songs like "We're Soldiers of the Queen, Me Lads" and "Duke's Son, Cook's Son" were clearer to Dorothy than the controversy over England's role in fighting the Boers. Nor, of course, could she have known that the war was a kind of rehearsal for the terrible First World War which engulfed her generation.

Dorothy spent time with her grandmother and her Aunt Leigh too. Aunt Leigh's parrot was the first of several that Dorothy knew and enjoyed, no matter how rudely they spoke or how loudly they yelled. Like her character Lord Peter, she had no time for a parrot without a salty personality.

Her Aunt Maud Leigh was a spinster. In the early 20th century not many jobs were thought proper for the unmarried daughters of the upper middle class. A lady without money might become a governess or teach in the girls' schools that were beginning to grow up, but there were few other white-collar jobs. Most spinsters lived in their richer relatives' homes. Their proper career was marriage, but for several generations in England there were more women than men. So it was customary for families to have these extra relatives living with them and helping to run the household and raise the children. They often took the children on trips, did odd jobs like the mending, and acted as nurse when someone was sick. Dorothy was always extremely fond of her aunt, who eventually came to live with her until she died.

While she was under ten Dorothy was taught by the gardener's son how to ride a pony and to speed skate on the long, curling Fen skates, but Dorothy played chiefly with her cousins when they came to visit, especially her cousin Ivy Shrimpton, who was her best friend until Dorothy went away to school. The two girls wrote each other long letters when they were apart. As an only child Dorothy was often alone or with adults.

She was also taken by her nurse or her family on Edwardian vacations by the sea, a great event before cars made such trips just a weekend excursion. First, the pony who pulled the trap, or small buggy, must be caught in the field. Since he was clever at avoiding work, the family was always anxious when there was a train to catch. Then there was a ride on the train with its steam engine and old-fashioned doors that opened out to the platform from every group of facing seats. Once at the seashore she might stay in a house or hotel, where they ate their meals in a dining room with other guests and could sit on a broad front porch and watch other vacationers going by. Dorothy's bathing suit was a woolly costume that reached from her neck to her knees and scratched, and she had a wooden pail and shovel to dig with in the sand.

Once on a trip like that with her nurse when she was quite small, Dorothy was watching the ocean waves come in when suddenly she realized that she was "herself," a person unlike anyone else—but that the same thing was true of others too. Many children's sense of their own individuality comes more gradually and is not so clearly remembered. But Dorothy got the idea like a clap of thunder and never forgot it, although when she told the grown-ups with her about her discovery, they accepted it matter-of-factly and responded, "Yes, of course, dear."

Dorothy's daily life was bound up in the religious duties and practices of a minister's family. Later, in one of her stories, she gives us a charming picture of what life must have been like in the Sayers rectory. Lord Peter and Harriet Wimsey are visiting the Dowager Duchess, Peter's mother. He asks Harriet if she minds going to church and she politely says no, but thinks to herself that it "felt a little odd . . . to stand . . . in the hall . . . waiting for a parent to come and shepherd one away to Morning Service. The Duchess came down, putting on her gloves, just as one's mother had always done, and saying,

"'Don't forget, dear, there's a collection today.'"

Lord Peter is asked to read the Bible lessons and, very like a minister, makes sure he has everyone's attention, stopping to look at a small boy and say,

"'Is that Willy Blodgett? Now, don't you pinch your sister again. It's not cricket.'"

"'There,'" said Willie Blodgett's mother in an audible whisper, 'Sit still! I declare I'm ashamed of you.'"

Dorothy was raised an Anglican, or Episcopalian, within the Church of England, which is the country's established church. Everyone in England at that time still belonged by law to a particular parish, and not too long before Dorothy was born, it was necessary to be a member of the Church of England even to vote, to go to the universities, or hold office. But the Church of England is not a state church, supported by government money. Its ministers are supported by tithes paid by their parishioners.

The Church of England was established during the Reformation and prided itself upon being the middle way between Roman Catholicism and Protestantism. Along with other Protestant churches, the Anglicans put great emphasis on the Bible, while like Roman Catholics, they had a set order of services and shared the ancient apostolic order of bishops. Within the Church practices in worship varied widely. Those who preferred less ceremony and only observed Prayer Book feast days were known as the Low or Broad Church group, while those who emphasized the service of Holy Communion (or Mass), private confession, and more elaborate vestments and rituals were High Church or Anglo-Catholics. All of them were bound together by their use of the Book of Common Prayer, which was written by Archbishop Cranmer during the reign of Edward VI, Queen Elizabeth's brother. It is one of the great treasures of the English language, together with the King James translation of the Bible and the plays of Shakespeare. All three were completely familiar to Dorothy. All Anglicans are traditionally orthodox in doctrine, and they subscribe to the historic creeds of Christianity.

Dorothy's family were neither High nor Low in practice, although some of Mr. Sayers' parishes, like the ones she describes in her books, were probably more Protestant than he would have liked. An example of this kind of attitude is shown in *The Nine Tailors* when Lord Peter admires the spectacular gilded angel roof of Fenchurch St. Paul's. The minister's wife cheerfully tells him it took ten years to convince their churchwardens that regilding the angels would not be going "straight over to Rome."

As a minister's child Dorothy participated in the life of the parish, going to church regularly, singing in the choir, saying her catechism and creeds, and learning to know the Bible and the Book of Common Prayer so thoroughly that as a writer she instinctively chose their phrases to help express her own ideas. Her father was shy about discussing religion with her personally, but his profession and personality made a lifelong impression upon her. She was both proud and fond of him. Although she was a young adult before she discovered that Christian theology could be exciting, the habits of her childhood kept her a practicing, if questioning, Christian during her adolescence. As a child Dorothy preferred stirring, martial church hymns to the sentimental ones often written for children. She liked to shout out hymns like "The Church's One Foundation," with its difficult words like "heresy" and "schism," as well as the ancient hymns like Palm Sunday's "All Glory, Laud and Honor."

Another important part of her upbringing was her acceptance of the unspoken "rules" about how one lived. She was raised like a boy to "play the game," which meant to keep a stiff upper lip, never cry in public, and never let your side down. Dorothy's real feelings she learned to hide, sometimes by deliberately overacting or clowning, sometimes by appearing not to care.

She read everything she could put her hands on, from classics by Dickens and Scott and Dumas and Kingsley, to children's books by E. Nesbit and Andrew Lang, to cheap magazine stories and boys' detective tales like the endless adventures of Sexton Blake, whom she called an English folk hero. Unlike many families, hers seems to have allowed her to read many books that were not usually thought suitable for children. She grew up in a house where books were all about, rather like C. S. Lewis' home in Ireland, where, as he said, there were books in the study, books in the drawing room, and books in the cloakroom and attic. One of Dorothy's classmates at Oxford, growing up in a more conventional home, was always given the latest Andrew Lang fairytale book for Christmas, but in her whole house there were only one or two other novels and a book on household medicine.

In the memories of many writers there is a private list of books which they read and reread when they were young and never forgot. These friends, who were often their best or only true friends, especially if they had no brothers or sisters, are always there in the backs of their minds, as familiar as their own homes and families and as much a part of their "real" life as anyone else.

The enormous number of books that Dorothy considered her special friends appear all through her own writings, and many of her characters quote from them. They range from Mother Goose to the poems of T. S. Eliot. As a girl she especially adored romantic adventure stories like *The Scarlet Pimpernel* or *The Three Musketeers* or *The Prisoner of Zenda*, while she also read the detective stories of Conan Doyle and Wilkie Collins and the stories of Edgar Wallace.

Whatever Dorothy read, she thought about and remembered. She made what she called "translations" from one story to another, helping herself to see new connections between things that seemed very different. In an amusing essay called "A Vote of Thanks to Cyrus," she explained that she once read about Cyrus, the ancient king of the Persians, in a children's magazine. There Cyrus was shown wearing a tunic like the Greek heroes in Kingsley's mythology book, so she decided that Cyrus's story must be a fairytale, because it had dreams and omens. But then Cyrus marched his army along the Euphrates River into Babylon, and she put him in history with the real Greeks and Romans.

But one day it occurred to her that Cyrus was also the Persian king who lived during Daniel's time and broke up the Babylonian feast with the handwriting on the wall; so he marched right out of history into the Bible. But Bible stories, she thought, belonged in church, not in real life, and Jesus, who should have been a link between the two, was talked about in a "church" voice and wore robes like a minister with a halo over his head. While she was still thinking about this problem, she read about Esther, who married Ahasuerus, another Persian king, who turned out to be really Xerxes, the Great King whom the Greeks fought at Thermopylae until they all were dead. Then at last Dorothy saw that history is all of a piece and the Bible is really a part of it.

3

THE POET

ABOUT 1905, WHEN DOROTHY WAS ALMOST THIRTEEN, her father hired a special French governess to teach her and some of the neighbors' daughters German and French. It was quite common to have such a special governess for a year or two to help young ladies learn to speak a foreign language fluently, and some girls were also sent to a finishing school in Switzerland before they made their debut into society. Dorothy was now expected to talk French most of the day. She learned how to read French very quickly and soon was enjoying Dumas' *The Three Musketeers*, which remained one of her favorite romances, along with the entire cycle of stories about King Arthur. She and her cousin Ivy liked to pretend that the rectory was really 17th century France and all its inhabitants characters from the book. Dorothy herself chose to be Athos, the most urbane and romantic of the three musketeers. By this time it was apparent that she had a special gift for languages, which her governess and her family encouraged.

Governesses themselves were part of a special social group. They came from middle-class families and some were very well educated, but they were neither quite members of the family nor, on the other hand, quite servants. Their place was with the children of the family, whose activities they took charge of and with whom they ate. Typically, a governess earned only about fifty pounds a year while a good cook got forty. Most of them were not particularly well educated in mathematics or science.

By the time she was fifteen Dorothy was fluent in both French and German, but she no longer liked Latin because, instead of being able to read novels and poems and plays, she had to work her way line by line through boring Latin classics like Cicero's speeches to the Roman Senate. After two world wars in which England has fought Germany, it seems strange that girls like Dorothy learned German, while in her grandmother's day ladies had learned Italian and read Dante and Petrarch. The German influence was caused partly by the British Royal family's close family connections with the German monarchy, which was overthrown after World War I.

Dorothy with her hair in pigtails down her back was confirmed, played her violin for church concerts, and helped her mother and aunt put on teas and jumble sales and pay calls on the parish. Like many of her contemporaries she also amused herself with writing. Dorothy did not keep a diary, but she kept notebooks at various times, and she always liked to write letters. Letter writing was a more common habit before the telephone came into daily use, and all her life Dorothy continued to write chatty, amusing letters, describing her life and work and entering into her correspondents' interests as if they were her own.

But being an adolescent is hard on both boys and girls. Dorothy called it the "poetic" age because, as she said, "It is self-centered; it yearns to express itself; it specializes in being misunderstood, it is restless and tries to achieve independence, and with good luck and good guidance it should show the beginnings of creativeness and a deliberate eagerness to know and do some one thing in preference to all others." Dorothy's preference already was to be a writer and she never changed her mind.

But teenagers need friends their own age who share their enthusiasms; and her best friend did not live nearby. Worst of all, for a very bright girl who had been educated like a boy, puberty itself brought the sudden, confusing proof that she was not so much a person as a female, born to have babies.

Many girls rejoice at growing up. They become fascinated by clothes, parties... and boys. But for a girl who was not particularly pretty, who had grown up thinking "like a boy," it was very upsetting to face the fact that she was only a girl. Even if Dorothy's own family did not make these assumptions—and they do not seem to have done so at all—there would be other people in the parish who would talk about how "odd" that tall, gawky, smart Sayers girl was.

Meetings for Women's Rights were causing public battles in the streets of London during Dorothy's adolescence, and Dorothy's parents may have been as sympathetic to their cause as the parents of her friend Charis Barnett, who took her to hear Mrs. Pankhurst, the Suffragette leader. But before the First World War of 1914 there was tremendous pressure on girls to catch a good husband, while only the extreme tactics of the Suffragettes were ever publicized, not their actual, legitimate aims. Worse yet, men were not supposed to like brains, and like any other adolescent girl, Dorothy also longed to be swept off her feet by Prince Charming.

Some of Dorothy's most interesting characters show the scars of this internal battle to grow up to be a person as well as a woman. Some, like the naive Vera Findlater or moody Ann Dorland, are very immature for their age. Feminist Eiluned Price, who snarls at Lord Peter when he tries to carry a tea-kettle for her, and even Marjorie Phelps, the "liberated" Chelsea artist, both have difficulty sorting out their own roles and relationships with men. And it is only when she can accept the idea that he cares about her as a person in her own right that Harriet Vane, the mystery writer, admits that she is wildly attracted by Peter.

When Dorothy was almost sixteen, her parents decided to send her away to boarding school. She needed expert teaching to pass the examinations for Oxford University, where she hoped to go. They also hoped she would enjoy school and make friends her own age. There were not many good schools for girls, and almost no schools were co-ed. These boarding schools for girls usually had headmistresses with a university education and made a point of hiring better educated teachers too.

In January 1909, Dorothy arrived at the Godolphin School in southern England. At first she was in a smaller house, or dormitory, called Oakhurst, but soon, because of her academic ability, she was put in Schoolhouse, the dormitory run by the headmistress, Miss Mary Alice Douglas. The school was located in the pleasant old cathedral town of Salisbury among the Wiltshire hills and had a much milder climate even in midwinter than the bleak Fens. Its famous cathedral, Old Sarum, and Stonehenge, with its primitive circle of monolithic rocks, were among the nearby places where the students were taken on excursions. The school enrolled about two hundred students, over half of them boarders. The rest lived nearby and came as day pupils.

Godolphin School was one of the less expensive of the girls' boarding schools, costing much less than the better-known Rodean, where Agatha Christie's sister went (Agatha herself was considered too shy and delicate for the rough and tumble of boarding school). It cost about five hundred dollars a year. Many of its students came from middle-class professional families such as lawyers and teachers. Everybody was limited to a pound (five dollars at that time) spending money a term, and their allowance was doled out to them by their housemistresses.

Instead of accepting the upper-middle-class ideal of marrying an acceptable young man, Godolphin students were encouraged to admire its graduates who had become a matron of St. Thomas Hospital in London or head of Girton College for Women at Cambridge University. Like most girls in those chaperoned days, Godolphin students had almost no chance to meet boys or get to know them unless they had brothers who brought their friends home during the holidays. But the girls usually enjoyed school and each other's company and were very sorry to leave.

Most of the students had come to Godolphin when they were twelve or thirteen, or at least had had the advantage of enrolling in the fall, when the school year began. When Dorothy arrived in January, she was nearly sixteen and much too old to adjust easily to being a new girl. She was not used to dormitory living with its lack of privacy, and she was tall and plain and lanky, with a long neck which made her fellow students nickname her "Swanny." She also had to wear spectacles for her nearsighted eyes, or otherwise squint.

Like C. S. Lewis, who so hated his boarding school that he finally had to be taken away and tutored privately, Dorothy had read boys' magazine stories about school life which made it sound jolly and fun. What she discovered instead was a highly organized group existence with many rules which she did not care for.

For example, when Godolphin's students marched into Hall for assemblies or when they walked into Salisbury to attend services at the Cathedral, they went two by two in a long line known as a crocodile. The older girls sometimes were allowed to go in groups of four. When the weather was fine, everybody in the school had to play team sports like lacrosse in winter and tennis and cricket in the summer. As in the boys' schools, a student's standing with her peers depended a lot on how good she was at games, and Dorothy loathed them. Since she had not played them since childhood, she was not much good at them either. Moreover, friendships had already been formed in her age group when she came, and there was no room for newcomers, so that although she tried to throw herself into the school activities, she remained an outsider.

Dorothy did not care much for wearing school uniforms all day and only a simple dress in the evenings. The Godolphin uniform was—and still is—a blue pinafore worn over a blouse and blue skirt. While Dorothy was there, their blouses still had stiff, starched collars like a man's, but during the First World War starch became so scarce that this discomfort finally ended. When they went out, the girls wore stiff straw hats with red ribbons and their long hair in plaits down their backs. The Upper Form girls put up their hair in a bun to show that they were considered grown up. All the girls had blue coats that matched their skirts, and underneath they wore warm underwear and long stockings to keep warm in the school buildings, which had no central heat. The girls got to wear shorter pleated tunics when playing sports. Although the Women's Rights movement included a fight for shorter, simpler clothing, it was only after the First World War that most women and girls bobbed their hair and chopped off their long skirts.

Not many Godolphin students cared about having careers, but Dorothy had been sent to Godolphin primarily to be sure she got into Oxford University, so it was her school work she attacked most vigorously. Her education had been very uneven because while she was excellent in English and modern languages, she knew very little mathematics. At first the school put her back several grades with girls much younger than she was. At the same time she astonished her schoolmates by translating a French sonnet into English *poetry* while they managed only a rough prose translation.

Miss Douglas, Godolphin's headmistress, was an awesome person with tremendously high standards, both academic and moral. She was very proud of being related to W. W. How, who had written the words to a number of hymns, among them "For All the Saints" and "Jesus, Name of Wondrous Love," and who later became a bishop. Under Miss Douglas, the religious atmosphere at Godolphin was both Low Church and evangelical. The name of God was spoken only in hushed whispers and careers were thought of as "service to others."

Miss Douglas always took school prayers herself and had her pupils recite daily the hymn "Come, Holy Ghost, our souls inspire and lighten with celestial fire." One of her favorite Bible readings to the girls was St. Paul's admonition to the Philippians: "Whatsoever things are true, whatsoever things are honest, whatsoever things are just, whatsoever things are pure, whatsoever things are lovely... think on these things." Dorothy found this pious and sentimental approach to Christianity most unattractive and disliked the total preoccupation with conduct and the deadly earnestness.

But by the fall of 1909 Dorothy had begun to fit into the school a little better. She had joined the Debating Society and become a student librarian. She wrote some French essays for the school magazine and became its editor. She also played the violin in the school orchestra and acted enthusiastically in the plays put on by Schoolhouse. Most of all, she had taken Miss Douglas' exhortation to study hard very seriously indeed, and as a result had been skipped to the top class, or highest form, in the school.

The English secondary school system used a series of standardized examinations which the students had to take to go from one level of school to another. It was especially important to get good scores on these examinations if a student wanted or needed a scholarship for college.

On Mark Reading Day, September 1909, Miss Douglas proudly announced to the school the results of the Oxford-Cambridge Joint Board Higher Certificate Examination. These were the top nationwide examinations for high school students who next would have to "sit for," or take, the actual university entrance examinations.

Godolphin School had gotten six full Certificates with Distinction, and three of the six had been won by one girl, Dorothy Sayers. By the fall of 1910, Miss Douglas was able to announce that Dorothy had passed Group B of the Cambridge Higher Local Examinations with Distinction in both

Written French and Spoken French and German. In fact, she had done better than any other candidate in England who had taken both language examinations.

But even with all these honors and the glory which she brought to the school, Dorothy was not very happy or popular. One reason for this is illustrated by her character Hilary Thorpe, the teenager in *The Nine Tailors*. In many ways Hilary is the kind of person Dorothy must have been at her age.

Hilary was a "red-haired girl of fifteen, dressed in black, tall and thin and rather gawky, though with the promise of becoming some day a striking-looking woman." "Striking-looking" is one of Dorothy's favorite phrases to describe her heroines. It is exactly what she herself had wanted to be because she knew she was not pretty and that she would never grow up to be beautiful.

Hilary has a very revealing talk with her father. He begins,

> "There'll be enough to send you to Oxford, I dare say. Girls don't seem to cost much there. . . .
>
> "Yes, and I'm going to get a scholarship, anyway. And I don't want money. I'd rather make my own living. Miss Bowler [her English teacher] says she doesn't think anything of a woman who can't be independent. I'm going to be a writer, Dad. Miss Bowler says she wouldn't wonder if I'd got it in me."
>
> "Oh! What are you going to write? Poetry?"
>
> "Well, perhaps. But I don't suppose that pays very well. I'll write novels. Best-sellers. The sort that everybody goes potty over . . . like *The Constant Nymph*."

Hilary's mention of that particular book is amusing because it is the tale of the talented but completely unconventional children of an expatriate English composer. After his death the heroine and her sisters are sent off to an English boarding school where they find the rules and life so impossible they run away. The book was written by Margaret Kennedy, a young contemporary of Dorothy's at Oxford. It was decidedly not the sort of book that Miss Douglas at Godolphin would have approved of her students reading.

It is easy to see why Dorothy had problems when Miss Douglas made her top student a house prefect, or student officer. She was still really a "new girl," but she had been given a job that gave her both power and responsibility. All her life, Dorothy was the kind of person who was better at running herself than she was at being in charge of other people—she expected too much of everybody.

Dorothy was determined to be the best prefect Godolphin ever had and make everything run according to the rules. To do this, she had to be bossy and that made her unpopular, particularly since she had a sarcastic way of talking. Then she tired of the job and let the house run itself, which was not much better.

Dorothy was taking piano lessons from a Fräulein Fehmer, who was German. The lessons were given in a row of little practice rooms down a dark passageway near the Fourth Form's classroom. Each little room was called by the name of a great composer, and Fräulein Fehmer's was named "Chopin," after her favorite. Sometimes she played Chopin for the students in Hall after supper. Dorothy said that what Fräulein Fehmer played was real music. There was a particular Chopin Nocturne that always reminded her of Godolphin's assembly room, its redbrick walls hung with games trophies, the rush-bottomed chairs the students sat in, and the row of plants along the edge of the platform where the music teacher, in an ugly dark silk dress, sat playing.

Fräulein Fehmer was stiff, with a square face and spectacles. She always wore a shawl over her shoulders and had her dark hair combed into a bun at her neck. When she started Dorothy on a new piece she wrote the date neatly at the top, and if Dorothy made a mistake, she would scold, "Na, na!" Dorothy found her rather frightening.

Much later, however, when Dorothy was a best-selling

author, Fräulein Fehmer wrote to her from Germany. She had heard that Dorothy was a writer and wanted to read one of her books but could not afford to order one from England. Dorothy began to send her copies of her novels as they came out, and they also exchanged polite Christmas cards until the Second World War began in 1939. Then Dorothy began to have nightmares about Fräulein Fehmer. She wondered if her teacher's passion for Chopin, who was Polish, had gotten her into trouble, if she had felt guilty when the Germans overran Poland; or she imagined Fräulein Fehmer maimed or killed by the heavy bombing in the major target area around Frankfurt. Finally, Dorothy wrote a poem called "Target Area," which ends on the bitter refrain,

> Chopin and the old School Hall were out last night over Germany... taking messages to Fräulein Fehmer.

In the spring term of 1911 a bad measles epidemic broke out at Godolphin and Dorothy caught them. Her isolated childhood had made her an easy victim, because she had not developed the proper immunities. After the measles, she got pneumonia and was left not only very weak but almost bald. She bought a wig and came back to school to finish the term, but found the effort too much for her. She became sick again and had to be sent to a nursing home in Salisbury. From there she went home to Bluntisham without ever going back to Godolphin School—so she did not actually graduate. The school was sorry to lose such a good student, but Dorothy did not feel any affection for Godolphin and never joined the Old Girls Association.

She studied for the university entrance examinations at home. During the year she made a trip by train to Oxford to be interviewed by the principal of the women's college she wanted to attend, which was called Somerville after a famous 18th-century woman scientist. Miss Emily Penrose was a majestic, intimidating sort of person, not at all the motherly type, who treated her students as much as possible as adults.

She fed prospective students like Dorothy tea on the lawn outside the main building and told them briskly what deficiencies they would have to make up to get into college.

Dorothy went again to Oxford to take the formal entrance examinations. She probably stayed in a student's room, cold and tiny, without hot water. The women's colleges at Oxford were only a generation old and had very small endowments, and so were poor and uncomfortable compared to many upper-middle-class homes or the men's colleges, with their elegant food and drink.

When the results of the tests came out, Dorothy had won one of the highest scholarships in England, one for which there was a great deal of competition. It was called the Gilchrist Scholarship, and its winner went to Somerville College, which was considered the toughest woman's college academically. The scholarship paid about fifty pounds a year, or about $250, which was enough to cover her major university expenses.

When asked, Dorothy said that neither her family nor the parish was greatly surprised when she was given the Gilchrist Scholarship because they had expected her to do very well! She herself remembered those important examinations with amusement because in one of them she showed off what she called her "congenital disease," her passion for translating verse from one language into another. She had taken the sonnet she was given to translate and done it in strict Petrarchan poetic form, making a new poem of it in the second language.

4

ALMA MATER

Dorothy had been born in the shadow of Tom Tower and had been brought up in the hope of calling herself an Oxford scholar, so when she entered the narrow gateway of Somerville College at the age of nineteen, it was like coming home. Oxford had not changed from the quiet city of her early memories, surrounded by open fields and pleasant villages. The total university population was only about three thousand people, of whom about 850 were new First Year students, men and women. After the university, the biggest employer in Oxford was the Oxford University Press, which had about 300 workers. Automobiles, which Oxford was to become famous for manufacturing, were almost unknown. There were horse-drawn buses, but nearly everybody rode bicycles.

When Dorothy arrived by train at the beginning of the Michaelmas, or fall, term in 1912, the women's colleges were still not officially part of the university, and the women students were not granted university degrees. This is why it is often said that Dorothy was one of the first women to get an Oxford degree. But there had been women students at Oxford for two generations before her, and she did not really think of herself as a pioneer. The fact they had studied at Oxford and passed the examinations required of the men gave the women great academic credit in the outside world and enabled them to get the top teaching jobs in girls' schools.

Still, many of the rights and privileges and quaint medieval customs that went with the men students were denied them, including the obligation to wear academic caps and gowns so that university officials like the proctors could tell at a glance which were students. The split between town and gown was still so great that to some extent the university policed its own students on the streets of the city. But as Dorothy described the situation, the women students "were not members of the University . . . it existed to set examination papers, to supply us with funny stories [and] a great tradition which was not ours. That tradition we faithfully followed, hoping that by our . . . make-believe we might somehow end by making the belief come true."

For the next three years, however, Dorothy went to lectures with the men, studied with many of the same tutors, and passed the same examinations. She had to take the same work as the men because Miss Penrose had adopted a policy of accepting only students who would work for honors degrees and pass all the necessary university examinations. As a result of her foresight, when degrees were finally granted to women, in 1921, Somerville College had the most graduates of all ages eligible to receive them.

In the meantime, the women's colleges did not encourage women's rights demonstrations in Oxford. If their students chained themselves to the gates of the vice-chancellor's home, the heads feared that the Oxford men (who must vote on the issue) would never grant women degrees. The women students were encouraged to follow the more diplomatic tack of showing how bright they were. Their battlefield was the examination hall, and Dorothy proved to be one of their best fighters. In fact, she went on the rest of her life operating in men's fields of work and proving herself their equal.

Somerville College had been founded in 1879 when the idea of higher education for women first became popular with liberal professors, clergymen, and politicians. It opened with only twelve shy students who lived in a private house along St. Giles Road on the edge of the university. The students were taken to lectures by pony cart and were always chaperoned. By the time Dorothy was a First Year student, or Fresher, there were a hundred students at Somerville and they were told to bring bicycles. All university lectures, coaching, and examinations were open to her, and chaperones were gone except for visiting in the men's colleges. But Dorothy could entertain only her father, uncle, or brother in her room, not other men friends. In many ways Somerville was still like a boarding school, with many regulations, such as the rule that students must be in their rooms by 11 p.m. Dorothy later commented sarcastically that it was hard to grow wise in a place where going to tea with a young man was considered a "thrilling dissipation." But the college was reflecting the social attitudes of the time and needed public approval to grow.

Thanks to the building campaign of the previous principal, Miss Maitland, Somerville College now had begun to resemble Dorothy's own invented Shrewsbury College, which had a

> stone quadrangle, built by a modern architect in a style neither old nor new, but stretching out reconciling hands to past and present. Folded within its walls lay a trim grass plot, with flower-beds splashed at the angles and surrounded by a wide stone plinth. Behind the level roofs of Cotswold slate rose the brick chimneys of an older and less formal pile of buildings—a quadrangle also of a kind, but still keeping a domestic remembrance of the original Victorian dwelling-houses that had sheltered the first shy students.

According to Dorothy's friend Muriel St. Clare Byrne, there was no such thing as a typical Somerville student. The college turned out students who were orthodox or unconventional, athletic or poetic, brainy or even social butterflies. But whatever point of view a student had about life, she could find someone at college who was ready to argue with her about it. Somerville students as a group were known to be intelligent and independent, not particularly fashionable, and their chief interest was their studies. In this atmosphere Dorothy quickly felt at home and became a leader of her Year.

College living for the women was not very elegant, and women and faculty members were not well paid. Like the men, the women had "scouts," or maids, assigned to a group of them. The scouts woke them in the morning, cleaned their rooms, and washed the dishes after parties. The dormitory rooms had washstands, a bed and a chest of drawers, as well as a coal fireplace and a gas ring for making tea. It was often chilly in college, especially in the larger public rooms and halls, and one student said she could see the don's words as he lectured because his breath made frozen puffs of air.

Until the new Maitland building with its college dining hall was finished in 1913, the students were housed in Hall, the original building, and West, with separate common rooms and dining rooms; a kind of rivalry existed between the two groups. The three main meals of the day were served in these residence halls, or later in the new dining hall with its portraits of principals and patrons on the paneled walls. They were waited on by the scouts except for Sunday night supper, which was always cold and called Nondescript, or Nondy. Student opinions varied on how good the food was, but it was never as good as the men's. Staple menu items were rice pudding and mutton.

Before breakfast the students were expected to shake hands with Miss Penrose, who then read prayers. But they could sit wherever they pleased in Hall, and some of them skipped breakfast completely or snacked in their rooms. College dinner was more formal. Students dressed up and had to get permission to be absent. They gathered in the Junior Common-room, which was shared by all Years as a kind of student lounge, and waited until a don arrived from the Senior Common-room, came up to a student, and escorted her to the dining hall. Then the Third Year students took in some Second Year students, and the rest were allowed to file in with their friends. They all sat at the long tables while the dons sat facing them at High Table. Then, "two hundred female tongues, released as though by a spring, burst into high, clamorous speech. . . . At the beginning of every term," Dorothy remarked, she "had felt that if the noise were to go on for one minute more, she would go quite mad. Within a week, the effect had always worn off." The dons addressed the students with the title "Miss," and the students did the same with one another until they had become friends.

By now Dorothy was not exactly "striking-looking," but she did stand out in a crowd. She was tall, about five feet seven, and still thin, and had the stride of a boy. Her straight dark hair had not grown out again after her pneumonia, so she wore a wig which she pinned on with a huge bow.

She also liked dramatic costumes. One morning she turned up in Hall for breakfast before going to a university lecture wearing a wide scarlet ribbon around her head and a pair of earrings that reached her shoulders, each one a tiny gilt cage with a red and green parrot inside. Looking down from High Table, the principal was appalled by Dorothy's appearance, but since it was against her policy to order students about in personal matters, she asked a poor Third Year student to try and coax Dorothy to take off the earrings.

Far from worrying about the world at large, which still thought that women students were odd females who would never marry, Dorothy entered into college life with all her usual zest and gusto, and fellow students felt that of all the pre-war Somerville students, Dorothy made the most lasting impression on her contemporaries and the world generally. Younger students liked Dorothy, too, because even as a lordly Third Year student, she was kind to Freshers and paid attention to them as individuals. They soon learned that they might bump into this bouncy, energetic person on the top floor of Maitland almost any hour of the day or night. Or she might be seen striding down the High, smoking, a habit many of the girls quickly took up to show they were now adult. She also cut lectures, which was perfectly legal and done by the men students all the time, but upsetting to Dorothy's tutors, who wanted their students to do brilliantly and get honors degrees.

Although tea was served every day in the Junior Common-room, the students liked to have tea parties in their rooms or midnight cocoa and coffee sessions. They learned that toasted marshmallows were cheaper than cream and tasted as good. The college provided them with bread and butter, while they could charge milk and pay their bill at the end of term. With their own money they bought whatever else they could afford at the moment, a pot of marmalade or biscuits or cake. Sometimes they invited dons to these parties, occasionally even the principal. One of Dorothy's friends who was particularly sociable brought from home a wooden fender for the fireplace to make extra seats.

The First Year students, excited by their freedom from rules about bedtime, as well as by the company of other girls with similar interests, often stayed up very late discussing life. Those who wanted to appear daring smoked cigarettes like Dorothy, largely because they could not, like the men students, go drinking in the many local pubs. Dorothy was known to be one of the college's night owls, and later, as an adult, she often worked late into the night.

In a college full of students who liked to have endless discussions on sex and politics and religion and art, Dorothy was soon known as one of the most eager and argumentative debaters. She and her friends later suspected that these midnight sessions had been the most valuable part of their college life.

One of Dorothy's favorite topics was religion, particularly Christianity. It was about this time that she began to consider its intellectual pattern and to develop her own rational approach to its official doctrines, unlike the more emotional and ethical attitude she had been taught at school. Largely through reading the novels and essays of the journalist G. K. Chesterton, who was an unconventional leader in defending orthodox Christianity before the First World War, Dorothy had begun to appreciate the fact that it made as much sense to be orthodox as it did to be a heretic. Chesterton defined heresy as the fashionable literary position of the day, held by such well-known writers as Rudyard Kipling, Bernard Shaw, and H. G. Wells.

Her participation in such discussions is reflected in an article she wrote about her friend Charles Williams in which she said that nothing was more startling than the changing attitudes towards Christianity in her lifetime. When she was a child, the bishops who doubted the resurrection of Christ were called courageous. When she was a girl, G. K. Chesterton said that he believed in the Resurrection and was called odd. When she went to Oxford, people who believed in the Resurrection were called advanced. By the time she was middle-aged, people who believed in the Resurrection were called courageous, and finally, when she was still older, anyone who, like her, wrote about Christianity was called an escapist and a bully, and people who attacked her were called courageous for doing so.

Dorothy herself felt a lifelong gratitude and affection for Chesterton, a generation older than she, whom she later knew personally. As she said,

> To the young people of my generation, G.K.C. was a kind of Christian liberator. Like a beneficent bomb, he blew out of the Church a quantity of stained glass of a very poor period and let in gusts of fresh air, in which the dead leaves of doctrine danced with all the energy and

indecorum of Our Lady's Tumbler.... It was stimulating to be told that Christianity was not a dull thing, but a gay thing... an adventurous thing... not an unintelligent thing, but a wise thing.... Above all it was refreshing to see Christian polemic conducted with offensive rather than defensive weapons.

There are even interesting parallels in her adult career and Chesterton's, for he too was famous for his bouncy personality and size, and wrote a wide variety of literature, from poems and essays and plays to detective stories.

Like her Shrewsbury College, Somerville was undenominational, but some form of Christian worship was held to be essential to community life. Miss Penrose, therefore, read prayers at breakfast in Hall. None of Dorothy's friends recalls her protesting, but then there is no evidence that she or her close friends ever broke a serious college or university regulation. They were having too good a time and none of them had any intention of being "sent down" from Wonderland.

People noticed Dorothy because she not only had a good musical voice, but a loud, clear, and distinct one, fit for the stage or the pulpit. She got into trouble right away for talking loudly in the Bodleian, Oxford's oldest library. Barbara Reynolds, a close friend of Dorothy, remembers taking her many years later into the library at Cambridge to look up a word. When Dorothy found it, she exclaimed clearly in a deep, resonant voice that startled everyone in the quiet reading room, "Here 'tis!"

With her musical background Dorothy naturally joined Oxford University's famous Bach Choir. There she learned the Latin mass and great choral works like Verdi's *Requiem* and ancient hymns like Peter Abelard's "O Quanta Qualia." The conductor of the Bach Choir was Dr. Hugh Allen, who later was knighted. Dr. Allen was famous for his exaggerated gestures while conducting and his rude manners. He had a reputation for saying whatever came into his head. Once he told a student who said she was a soprano but wanted to sing alto that she was the cantankerous type who would want to sing soprano if she had been born an alto. Such manners frightened off the shy students, but Dorothy loved it. She developed a crush on Dr. Allen, which she never tried to hide. Instead she sat during practices gazing at him with wide, adoring eyes, while the rest of the choir made jokes about her. But Dorothy knew she was being ridiculous, and in her Third Year she had the last word.

Amateur theatricals were very much a part of college life. Somerville students went to see plays put on by other colleges in the university and by OUDS, the Oxford University Drama Society; they also produced plays themselves. Dorothy and her close friends took part in many of them. In their First Year, two of her friends, Dorothy Rowe and Charis Barnett, played Hamlet and Horatio in a take-off on *Hamlet* called "Hamlet, the Pragger Dagger," which was the slang title for the Prince of Wales, who was then at Oxford. Second Year, their class put on both "Admiral Guinea," stage-managed by Dorothy Rowe, and "Prunella," for which Charis Barnett designed the Statue, using her electric bicycle light.

Then in their Third Year they followed college tradition and wrote and gave a "Going Down" play, which was put on in the dull time between their final examinations and leaving for good. The Going Down play was a kind of "family" musical comedy that only Somerville could really understand, full of silly jokes and comments about college life. The plays were never greatly artistic, but they were lots of fun, full of popular tunes with new words.

In 1915 the Going Down play was called "Pied Pipings: or The Innocents Abroad." Its plot turned about the fact that the poor Third Year students were having a terrible time because their professors kept making up new theories about their subjects. The Pied Piper then transported all the dons to

Never Land, where they met dead subjects like Shakespeare and discovered that their theories were completely wrong. The dons did not care for this and wanted to go back to Oxford at once, but the Piper told them that now they were dead too and that the students were busy making up theories about them!

The songs were set to tunes from Gilbert and Sullivan, and Dorothy both directed the musical and played the leading role. She was the Pied Piper himself, called Dr. H. P. Rallentando (which is a musical term for slowing down), and she not only imitated Dr. Allen of the Bach Choir with his wild gestures, but she made herself up to look like him. A picture of herself in this costume hung on the wall of her study at Witham.

Dorothy's Gilchrist Scholarship paid her basic college fees. Beyond that, she undoubtedly was about as poor as her character Harriet Vane, who is not amused by Lord Peter's rich nephew Lord St. George, who is always broke and borrowing from his uncle. Harriet Vane had about five pounds (or twenty-five dollars) a term to make whoopie on, while Dorothy may have had no more than her friend Charis, who got about two pounds per term.

Fortunately, Oxford offered many enjoyable activities that did not cost much money. Some of Dorothy's friends and classmates who liked team sports played hockey or tennis for Somerville, wearing white blouses and skirts a daring twelve inches off the ground, with a tie of Somerville's red and black colors. (During final examinations the principal was asked to keep the young ladies from exposing their ankles because it distracted the men.)

There were also many charming places to bike or walk to about Oxford, and the students had picnics with sandwiches and coffee which they got from the College buttery (kitchen). Dorothy and the other Freshers were taken on the river in the college's old outrigger, the *Urmila*, until they passed the water test. Then they could use the punts and canoes to spend lazy afternoons reading or daydreaming along the banks. There were university festivals too, such as hearing the Magdalen College choir, which sang a medieval hymn at sunrise on May Day, when those who had gotten tickets could also climb Magdalen Tower, with its square, pinnacled roof. The biggest holiday at Oxford was Eights Week, when the colleges had their famous boat race up the river and many families and visitors came.

Hundreds of different clubs and societies appeared and disappeared at both the men's and women's colleges. Some were sports clubs, dining clubs, drinking clubs, or political clubs, but many of them were interested in literature or philosophy.

In November 1912, when they were in their First Year, Dorothy and some of her friends started a literary club which they called the Mutual Admiration Society, or M.A.S. Dorothy told them that if they didn't call the club by that name, the rest of the college certainly would. M.A.S. had only about a dozen members, all but three of them from their Year, even though it became well known and some older students tried to join. New members were voted in after old members had read a piece of the candidate's writing. In May 1914 they voted to take in a First Year student named Muriel St. Clare Byrne, who became one of Dorothy's best friends.

The M.A.S. met after dinner one night a week in a member's room to read their creations aloud for mutual entertainment and criticism. All kinds of literature were produced, from poems to plays to parts of novels. One member wrote a witty dialogue between Dr. Johnson and his biographer Boswell on women's right to vote, while Dorothy once read aloud a conversation among the Three Wise Men. All of the members except Amphilis Middlemore, who died young, published books when they were adults, and a number of them published things in university magazines. Charis Barnett and Dorothy

Rowe both had poems in *Oxford Poetry 1914*, while Dorothy contributed one called "Lay" in *Oxford Poetry 1915*. Dorothy also published two poems in the *Oxford Magazine*—"Hymn in Contemplation of Sudden Death," and "Epitaph for a Young Musician." Another of her poems, about Tristan and Isolde, was published in the women's intercollegiate magazine called *The Fritillary*.

Among the M.A.S. membership were a number of people who remained Dorothy's close friends all her life. From her own Year there was Dorothy Rowe, who became a teacher in a girls' school in Bournemouth, who in turn was usually to be found with Charis Barnett, a tall, dark girl whose father was a well-known educator. He objected to the fact that after Oxford, Charis insisted upon going into midwifery instead of teaching. Muriel St. Clare Byrne was a year younger than the rest. An only child, she had grown up in Liverpool with her mother, who was an American whom her father had met on Pike's Peak in Colorado. After her father's death, her grandfather lived with them. One of Muriel's best friends in her Year was Marjorie Barber, who also became Dorothy's friend, and was older than the rest because she had been ill with TB. Marjorie too was tall and dark, while Muriel was a small, quick, talkative girl with a sense of humor to match Dorothy's own. Margaret Chubb, who like Charis Barnett became concerned about public health as an adult, and the novelist Muriel Jaeger were other members of M.A.S. Dorothy's friend Helen Simpson was also at Oxford during the war, but she and Dorothy did not become acquainted until the 1930s. Helen came up to study music as a Home Student in 1915, but took a pass degree in French in 1916 instead. Both Marjorie Barber and Helen Simpson shared Dorothy's interest in Christianity, while Charis Barnett married her Jewish second-cousin, Sydney Frankenburg, and somewhat to her mother's dismay, was very open about his religion.

Oxford abounded in debating societies, and Dorothy participated in several of them. One was known as "Parliament" and was modeled after the actual English government. Many women students learned to speak there. Dorothy was known in college as a good debater who always stuck to the point.

In spite of all these activities, Dorothy and her friends were serious about their work and often spent six hours or more a day studying. They were closely watched by their tutors, and during vacations they were assigned papers to write on what they had been studying. At the end of every term they had to get their reports from Miss Penrose and hear her comments about them.

The academic year at Oxford was divided as it had been in medieval times into three six-week terms called Michaelmas (fall), Hilary (winter), and Trinity (spring). There was a "vac" of a month between Michaelmas, Hilary, and Trinity. Then there was the long "vac" between Trinity and Michaelmas.

Dorothy had chosen to "read," or study, Modern Languages, which was one of the "Schools," or major subjects, in which a student was given a Bachelor of Arts degree. Any language which appeared after Latin and Greek was considered "modern," and Dorothy actually specialized in medieval French. But first she had to pass a series of examinations in Latin, Greek, mathematics, and Bible.

The colleges were chiefly residences for the students, or junior members, and the dons, or senior members, who were the fellows, tutors, and professors. The university granted degrees, based on its examinations, even though no student actually attended Oxford University as such. When Dorothy was a student, most of the women students came from middle-class families, and a number came on scholarships or grants. All students were either Scholars, Exhibitioners, or Commoners, and the men students in each group wore different kinds of academic gowns. Scholars were the brightest students, like Dorothy, who had won the biggest awards; Exhibitioners like J. R. R. Tolkien had not done quite so well; the Commoners were simply students who paid their own way. An earl might easily be a Commoner at Oxford.

All students studying a "school" had to take the same lectures and examinations, and then take a final examination called Schools, which determined the degree granted them. The honors degrees were First Class, Second Class, etc.; those students who did not take honors got a pass degree.

Her First Year Dorothy was sent to Mr. Herbert May to be crammed through Responsions, or Smalls, the Latin and Greek examination. He lived in the gloomier part of Oxford and perpetually took snuff during his coaching sessions. He found many of Dorothy's translations unintentionally amusing, but he told her that at least she did write Latin, by which he meant that she knew how to put a Latin sentence together. Dorothy remembered only enough Latin to pass the examination; the same with Greek. Then she promptly forgot them to stick to French and German. After her first term she also had to pass an examination called Divinity, or "Divvers," which many of the brightest students failed and had to take a second time, often barely passing even then.

Dorothy was then assigned to a chief tutor at her college, who met with her once a week. The tutor would assign Dorothy a paper to write on the reading she was doing by herself, and then the next week would tear the essay apart, criticizing her style, her structure, and her facts. Some tutors were very sarcastic as they did this, but Dorothy's chief tutor, Miss Mildred Pope, was a kindlier sort.

Mildred Pope was born in 1872 into a poor minister's large family. In her portrait which hangs in Somerville's dining hall, she has a plain, humorous face with intent, bespectacled eyes under tightly combed hair and rather dowdy clothes. In her spare time she loved to play hockey.

In 1920 Miss Pope was the first woman don to be appointed a university lecturer, and in 1934 she was appointed to the chair of Romance Philology (modern languages) at

Manchester University. To become a professor was a great accomplishment in England, where there is usually only one professor for each subject at any university; few women get that kind of recognition.

In 1935 at a Somerville College Gaudy Dinner, or alumnae banquet, Dorothy was there to propose the formal toast to the university, and in her speech she paid special tribute to Miss Pope, saying,

> She has always seemed to typify some of the noblest things for which the University stands. The integrity of judgment that gain cannot corrupt, the humility in the face of the facts that self-esteem cannot blind; the generosity of a great mind that is eager to give praise to others; the singleness of purpose that pursues knowledge as some pursue glory. . . . Mildred Pope would be the first to say that Oxford made her what she is; we say that it is the spirit of scholarship like hers that has made Oxford anything at all.

There were a number of other outstanding dons at Somerville while Dorothy was there. The principal, Miss Penrose, had been the classics tutor, while the English tutor, Miss Darbishire, later became principal. She was known to appear asleep as she listened to an essay, then awake to give a detailed criticism of the paper. Miss Lorimer, the classics tutor, was a peppery redheaded Scot who biked and birdwatched and was blunt to dull students.

Being a don was a lifework, and most of these women did not marry. Typically, they lived very quiet, disciplined lives, devoted to their students and their studies, and that may have influenced Dorothy's continued determination to have a nonacademic career. In fact, none of her close friends at Oxford was to become a university don. But of all the women Dorothy knew, she admired these university women perhaps the most.

Her attitude about them is best summed up in her novel *Gaudy Night*, whose title comes both from the official name used for alumnae gatherings and from Shakespeare's *Antony and Cleopatra*. *Gaudy Night* is the one book which most women graduates find expresses their own feelings about their university education, because it conveys the atmosphere, the joys, the problems, and the people in a loving but realistic way.

Harriet Vane, the heroine, returning to Oxford like Dorothy herself after a number of years when she had to struggle to earn a living, echoes Dorothy's own ironic comments on the "younger generation." She has little patience with students who have allowed themselves to be bullied into coming to "waste three years which are unlike anything else in one's lifetime." At the same time, Harriet, who has sided with London against Oxford, comes to see that the ordered tranquility of the university is not something abnormal or unreal which can easily be destroyed.

One of the threads of the plot itself is the problem of women running a strictly female institution. It asks whether such a society is "healthy." The answer is that Dorothy did not regard its somewhat cloistered, or segregated, community as neurotic or unproductive. In fact, the women's colleges were no more so than the men's, where dons like C. S. Lewis spent most of their time associating with students or other congenial male colleagues.

Gaudy Night makes a moving plea for the importance such places have for society as a whole. They are the still centers where men and women can live self-examined lives, "translating" ideas and concepts into other terms and testing them for truth. Dorothy's whole adult personality was shaped by Somerville College and it gave her a sense of worth as a person. She in turn became a missionary to the outside world, who proclaimed the importance of teaching men and women to think for themselves.

When World War I broke out on August 4, 1914, Dorothy was in France on vacation, and she had the scary experience of nearly being trapped there. Trains were being commandeered to move troops to the front and the cross-Channel boats were jammed with returning vacationers. When she did get back to Oxford, it was already in the middle of wartime changes and the young men were disappearing into the army. At first there were only parades and drills; then, as the casualties mounted, the colleges were turned into military hospitals. Between 1914 and 1915 the number of men at Oxford dropped from 3000 to 1000, and soon few of them were left.

The colleges tried to persuade the young women to carry on as usual. Women's rights in general were helped by the war, for many university-educated women filled important jobs in the place of men. But only a few undergraduates like Vera Brittain and Winifred Holtby, both writers, quit to volunteer as nurses. When they came back, Miss Penrose treated them as if they had been playing hookey.

It is not surprising that Dorothy, who was in her Third and Final Year, did not quit to be a heroine. In any case her eyesight was so bad she would not have been allowed to go overseas. But the homefront also suffered in many ways, from strict food rationing and shortages and blacked-out cities to the dreadful, continuous grief over casualty lists in which the men from whole towns were wiped out in a single battle. Dorothy's Oxford poetry shows that her mind, like everyone else's, was on war and death for the young.

Somerville College was also taken over as a hospital and the students moved into parts of Oriel College for the duration. This move into a men's college produced wisecracks from the newspapers and silly games on the part of some male students who actually tried to tunnel into the girls' living quarters one night.

Just before Somerville gave up its new buildings for the war effort, the students had a farewell party and played the popular game of "Murder," a detective version of hide and seek. Those who were there later recalled that the chief clue had been finding a naked body in a bathtub, the same situation which opens Dorothy's first mystery, *Whose Body?* But for the most part, it was a tense, unhappy time in Oxford, where Great Tom's nightly boom was silenced so the German bombers could not find the town, while the other church bells called the entire university to prayers every noon.

During her Third Year Dorothy tried again to be an administrator. She was made Somerville's bicycle secretary. Bicycles were a constant nuisance—knocking over old dons, left all over, borrowed and not returned. Dorothy solved the problem by having all the bikes left about impounded. Their owners got them back only after they paid a fine which was sent to the Red Cross. As usual, Dorothy was too efficient for popularity, and behind her back the students began to call her the "Bicycle Tyrant."

True to her sense of humor, which was always her saving grace, Dorothy had the last word on bicycles, too. In the same Going Down play in which she made fun of herself for being in love with Dr. Allen, she also sang a song to the tune of "I've got a little list," from *The Mikado*. It was called the "Bicycle Secretary's Song," and it listed all the things she had been accused of doing at college, from arguing all night, whispering loudly in the library, and whistling Bach and Verdi in the quad, to being overzealous about bicycles.

Through all this confusion Dorothy had to study for the Final Honors examinations or Schools. At the best of times, many students found it terrifying to take examinations in everything they had studied for the past three years, then wait a month while the examinations were read by the dons. After that, they had to go before a panel of the professors for their *viva voce,* or oral examination. This oral often determined whether or not one got a First or Second Class Honors, and many students were too nervous to do well.

But the natural dramatic instincts which later made Dorothy a superb lecturer stood her in good stead at this time. She sailed through all her written examinations and shone in her orals too. The university examiners went out of their way

to say that they felt her French prose composition was unsurpassed in elegance, gaiety, and style.

She took First Class Honors in Modern Languages, specializing in French, thus ending her Oxford career on the same high note with which she had begun. Still, the satisfaction of success was tinged with sadness and regret at leaving Oxford. In a poem published a year later in 1916, she expresses her feelings poignantly:

> *Now that we have gone down—have all gone down,*
> *I would not hold too closely to the past,*
> *Til it become my staff, or even at last,*
> *My crutch, and I be made a helpless clown.*
>
> *Therefore, God love thee, thou enchanted town,*
> *God love thee, leave me, clutch me not so fast;*
> *Lest, clinging blindly we but grope aghast,*
> *Sweet friends, go hence and seek your own renown,*
> *Now that we have gone down—have all gone down.*

And anyone who loved college life can sympathize with the quiet farewell of her poem called "Last Morning in Oxford":

> *Like Homer with no thunderous rhapsody,*
> *I closed the volume of my Odyssey...*
> *The thing that I remember most of all*
> *Is the white hemlock by the garden wall.*
>   *June 23, 1915*

5

DOMINA

"THE HATRED OF WORK MUST BE ONE OF THE MOST depressing consequences of the Fall," wrote Dorothy. So far she had never failed to give every ounce of energy and enthusiasm she had to her work of getting an education. Now she was twenty-two years old and had to begin to support herself and prove the value of her education. Although her First Class Honors degree meant that she could have become a don, the number of women hired to teach at the university level was small and their salaries low. Then, too, their energies were supposed to go into teaching and writing scholarly books to build up an academic reputation. Something about the whole profession sounded too restricted to Dorothy, who liked to think of the whole world "as her oyster," as the old saying goes. In that respect she was like her close college friends, many of whom had varied careers involving several different kinds of work.

She had already determined to be a writer and needed to find the best way to support herself while she worked at her writing. Before starting her first job, she went back home to the Fens, where she found that the life of a rector's daughter at home was boring and that parish affairs took up a lot of time. But while she was home she worked at some writing projects which reflected the way she hoped to earn her living someday.

At Oxford she had begun a verse translation of the epic *Song of Roland* and had shown it to Miss Pope. *Roland* is the story of King Charlemagne's nephew, who is killed defending the rear of his uncle's army at Roncevaux. It is written in medieval French. Miss Pope had told her that this translation had "promise," but Dorothy left it unfinished to begin another Old French project, this time translating a version of the story of the star-crossed lovers Tristan and Isolde. She also spent many an afternoon just lazing about, rereading Sherlock Holmes and Edgar Wallace, writing poetry, or hiking along country roads to stop and sit on a gate and smoke a daring cigarette. About this time, too, when the war news generally was very bad, she heard that her friend Charis' only brother had been killed. Charis had asked the Friends War Victim Relief Committee how to get overseas herself, only to be told to go and train to be a midwife first. She proceeded to do so, and after six months' training went to France and worked in a maternity hospital near the front lines.

For her first job, Dorothy chose to do what most Oxford women graduates did: she got a job teaching in a girls' school. Some of her classmates found such teaching jobs dreadful. They had to deal with rigid, bossy principals, and many of their students were not interested in school, while the other teachers were often suspicious of the university graduates.

In many ways Dorothy seems to have been a good teacher. Her first job was as the Modern Languages Mistress, or teacher, at Hull High School for Girls. Hull is an important seaport which handles much of the trade with northern Europe. Dorothy lived on a pleasant residential street and did not have to live in the school with institutional duties day and night. Hull was a rich city, and since Dorothy was always fascinated by architecture, she enjoyed exploring Holy Trinity Church and St. Mary's, where a pathway runs through the tower, walking streets with names like the Land of Green Ginger, or seeing the medieval mansion of the De La Pole family of wool merchants.

Dorothy never wrote a story about being a teacher, but when she became a popular lecturer, she talked a lot about education. Some of her pupils remembered her because she was different from the other teachers. She was attractive and young and dressed well and moved quickly. They liked her deep laugh that matched her amused grin when someone made a funny mistake in class. She got them to do things they had never tried before, from writing verses in Latin to doing plays in French. One of her classes put on a Molière play for a Red Cross benefit. She also recruited and organized a school choir by moving about during assembly, listening while the girls all sang and then picking out the ones she wanted instead of taking volunteers.

Meanwhile in 1916, when she was twenty-three, Dorothy had a real triumph. Her first volume of poetry, called *Op I* (or first work in Latin), was published in Oxford by Basil Blackwell. It was a slim brown volume bound in limp leather and was Number 9 in a series called "Adventurers All, A Series of Young Poets Unknown to Fame." Dorothy dedicated the book to her special friends and associates of her college days—"the Stage-Manager of Admiral Guinea [Dorothy Rowe], the Conductor of the Bach Choir [Hugh Allen] and the Members of the Mutual Admiration Society"—telling them that "Many a true word is spoken in jest."

A number of the poems had been published before. They are all about college or about heroic people like King Arthur or Trojan Paris and Helen. Many reflect concern about the war, although one is a short poem about the Three Wise Men and another is an interesting account of Jesus Christ and Judas Iscariot meeting at the Gates of Paradise. They are full of the nostalgia for lost youth typical of recent graduates, but one is her challenge to the future as a writer and craftsman:

> *I will build up my house from the stark foundations,*
> *If God will give me time enough,*
> *And search unwearying over the seas and nations*
> *For stones or better stuff.*

MAKER AND CRAFTSMAN

Though here be only the mortar and rough-hewn granite,
I will lay on and not desist
Til it stand and shine as I dreamed it when I began it,
Emerald, amethyst.

Basil Blackwell took the future of English literature very seriously. He decided that its new writers must come from the university-educated middle class who survived the war. While many of the young poets he encouraged did turn out to be famous writers, almost none of them did so as poets. Most of them were novelists like Aldous Huxley or Charles Morgan. At this time, they were all, like Dorothy, trying to earn a living and find enough time to write.

By 1917 Dorothy had become convinced that teaching was a mistake for her professionally, because it was too demanding. Aldous Huxley, another "Adventurers All" poet, was a great success when he taught at Eton, but he quit because he had no time for his own writing. Dorothy finally quit her job too, and went back home for a while, where her father had just traded parishes with the rector of Christchurch near Wisbech. His new job paid him less than his old one, and his new church was an ugly one made of redbrick and designed by a railroad station architect. This parish was still deeper into the Fens, not even on a decent road.

The Christchurch minister had a large family and probably needed more money, while the Christchurch parish was smaller and less work for an elderly man like Mr. Sayers. The new rectory still had room for Mr. Sayers to have his study, Aunt Leigh and her parrot their sitting room, and Mrs. Sayers her den. Dorothy also had a bed-sitting room, facing a clump of trees. She moved into it all her detective stories, her school books, her childhood favorites, and a large pile of *Op I*, which had not sold very well. The Christchurch parish had not known Dorothy and were critical and gossipy about her habits. They were dismayed by a rector's daughter who spent hours reading novels in her room or walked about smoking.

Fortunately, Dorothy soon had a new job.

It was back in Oxford, where Dorothy felt she really belonged, and it was the kind of job that seemed to fit her ambitions better than teaching did. Basil Blackwell, her publisher, had hired her to work for his company. She was to be one of his readers while she learned the printing trade. Dorothy stayed at the new rectory only long enough to arrange for some cheap rooms in Oxford and happily departed again.

For a young woman of twenty-four, though, Oxford in 1917 was a sad place. The war was still going endlessly on, and what students were left were living in lodgings about town. There were almost no men at all except the hospitalized veterans. Dorothy rejoined the Bach Choir, which gave concerts to the patients in hospitals. She was surprised to discover that the older patients often chose gloomy hymns instead of the rousing cheerful ones she preferred.

Dorothy threw herself into her work at Blackwell's, where she gained a reputation for being merry, talkative, and, as usual, quick to jump into an argument over ideas. But the daily work of copy editing and printing, in which she learned to check spelling and punctuation, to catch errors, and to read and evaluate other people's manuscripts did not suit her. As Basil Blackwell said later, it was like harnessing a racehorse to a plow.

Dorothy did not waste her time at Blackwell's. Later on she edited several anthologies of detective stories and she knew and used all the tricks of the trade in regard to the production of books. She typically used printer's marks to edit her own copy.

Meanwhile Dorothy had little money, because her job was an apprenticeship for which she was paid partly by being taught the trade. Her family sent her a small allowance to help pay her room and board, and to save cleaning expenses she wore plain dark dresses. But she clung to her early love of long earrings and brightly colored beads, and occasionally she wore something outrageous, such as the time she sewed a red rose on the front of her dress and put one on her hat to match.

While she was working in Oxford she published some poems in various Oxford magazines and in the *London Mercury*. Beginning in 1917, Dorothy was also one of the co-editors (and the first woman editor) of Blackwell's yearly edition of *Oxford Poetry*. In 1919 one of her co-editors was the poet Siegfried Sassoon, and during this time she also worked with Aldous Huxley and the Sitwell brothers on a volume of poetry. Amusingly enough, in *Oxford Poetry 1918* there was a sassy poem on the W.R.N.S. (the Women's Royal Naval Service) by Helen Simpson following a long one by Dorothy on *Pygmalion*.

Living in Oxford again, Dorothy met several people who became friends, among them Doreen Wallace, who was a Second Year student at Somerville and lived near Dorothy in Bath Place. In a letter she sent to *The Times* after Dorothy's death, Doreen gave a clear, amusing picture of her energetic post-graduate friend, bouncing about her native heath again. She commented that she had never known anyone so brimful of the energy of a well-stocked mind, but that Dorothy had a lighter side too. Among a number of activities, the two of them helped organize the Rhyme Club, whose members were given one minute to come up with a rhyming line, sensible or nonsense.

Along with their effort to succeed as writers, the group of young people Dorothy associated with was trying to work out its own moral and ethical values. The war had changed the secure, stable, but stuffy world of their childhood, and many of them were idealistically determined to create a "brave new world" in its place. The social revolution demanding "free love" entered society with the war, when for those of Dorothy's age and younger all ideas of right and wrong were impaired by the awful understanding that they must grab what they could today, for tomorrow they might be dead. The life expectancy of a young officer in the army was two weeks, and everyone Dorothy knew had lost friends and relatives—or, like her friend Charis, were marrying soldiers who probably would not return. Their frantic search for pleasure lasted into peacetime, when the survivors came home, tired and wounded, to find serious economic problems which often meant they could not find jobs.

Educated people were also beginning to read Freud and other psychologists who first dealt with the issues of freedom and repression in clinical terms. Trying to follow these new ideas in practice, they often imitated the lifestyle of "Bohemia," which was the name given to the casual society of young artists and musicians who lived in garrets, originally in Paris, and struggled to go on painting and composing.

The great fight for women's rights had also helped to make the young women of Dorothy's generation feel that they must be as free in their behavior as men traditionally had been. Obedience to the Christian rule of chastity had never been fully expected of men, who were allowed to enjoy themselves in sexual adventures, then marry some "nice" girl and settle down. Now the nice girls wanted the adventures too, even though their parents' generation was highly disapproving. They did not want to sit home and wait to be swept off their feet, and the brightest and most educated felt that they might never marry, since marriage was too demanding if one wanted a real career as well. Then too, there was an even greater than usual surplus of women in England as a result of the war.

Most of Dorothy's generation were unsophisticated about sex itself. Their only experience of being in love was in the form of school girl crushes or a distant passion like Dorothy's for some older, unattainable man like Dr. Allen. When Dorothy returned to Oxford, she still had very little chance to see a young man by herself and carry on a normal conversation. The university still frowned on public meetings between the sexes, and both men and women could be sent down for visiting in each other's rooms.

Meanwhile the young men who returned from the war were finding that the changing attitudes meant that they could, if they wished, be even more demanding and give less in return. Some girls in this situation were able to take care of themselves, some were just lucky.

Dorothy, who never did things by halves, fell in love with one of the most attractive veterans in Oxford, a tall, elegant young officer named Eric Whelpton. He had been invalided home from France and had come up to Oxford in 1919 to finish his university education when he was twenty-four and Dorothy was just twenty-five. Other young women were also interested in him, among them Dorothy's new friend Doreen Wallace, who introduced them.

Eric Whelpton was both bright and well educated. He came from a well-off, middle-class family with aristocratic friends and connections abroad, and he liked to think of himself as a "European." In fact, through his mother's family he had a claim to an ancient title from the old Holy Roman Empire, a fact that Dorothy would have found romantic. He could afford to entertain his friends well and bought his clothes in the expensive London shops of Saville Row and Jermyn Street.

With his smooth dark hair and English good looks and background, Whelpton was close to Lady Mary Wimsey's very Europeanized fiance Denis Cathcart in *Clouds of Witness*. But Whelpton himself liked to think that he was actually the model for Lord Peter Wimsey. Ironically, he disliked mystery stories and never finished a single one of Dorothy's.

Whelpton found Dorothy's company and conversation very entertaining, and he let her "reeducate" him after four dreary years of war. Some of the writers she introduced him to were her favorite 17th-century poets, like John Donne and Robert Herrick. They met several times a week, but always with other people about, and he claimed that he never realized that Dorothy was in love with him. Since he was in love with another woman, it is possible he took Dorothy's attention for granted, not having Lord Peter's ability to be aware of such situations and handle them gracefully.

But it was a difficult situation for Dorothy. She and Blackwell's had agreed that she was not cut out to work on other people's writing when she wanted to write herself. In 1918, as if to emphasize her dilemma, since she had not been able to earn her living as a writer either, Blackwell's put out her second book of poems, called *Catholic Tales and Christian Songs*.

Like her first book, it did not sell well, but it is interesting to read because it foreshadows some of her later writing and shows how her original interests were to remain with her all her adult life. Most of the poems reflect a religious concern, often about vocation, and some of them have strong echoes of G. K. Chesterton as well as of Chesterton's ironic Roman Catholic friend Hilaire Belloc. Written in modern speech, the poems reveal a young writer hunting for a Christian use of her talents in the bleak postwar world. They undoubtedly would have shocked her father's parishioners.

About 1920, when Whelpton went down from Oxford and took a job at the Ecole des Roches in Normandy, France, Dorothy gave up her own job although she and Basil Blackwell remained good friends. She went home again. Her family allowed her to continue writing in her own room, but it was not the same as being independent, and by now she, like her contemporaries, knew that she could not make a living writing poetry.

Then she received a job offer from Eric Whelpton that proved he had recognized her as a capable, intelligent woman. The French school where he was working had asked him to set up an office for international academic exchanges, and he wrote to ask Dorothy if she would come to help him run it. The Ecole des Roches was a famous institution, a cross between an English Public School like Eton and the more rugged, sports and outdoor activity-minded Gordonstoun, where the British royal family has sent its sons recently.

Dorothy did not jump at the offer; neither did she turn it down. She may or may not have known that Eric Whelpton was engaged to a young woman in London who was very ill, but working with him was very appealing. It was also a chance to be independent and might be the kind of job in which she would have time to write. Before she accepted, she invited Whelpton to come to Christchurch to meet her parents, and soon afterwards she was installed in the French school. The two lived in different buildings, but they worked together in the same office twenty or thirty hours a week.

Their jobs were not very demanding and they had plenty of time to talk and work on their own projects. Whelpton began to realize that Dorothy was reading all kinds of detective stories. When he teased her about reading trash, she offered to let him join her in a project. She told him that she and some other friends were going to make detective stories fashionable reading for intelligent people and make their fortunes while they were at it. At the time, the market for mysteries was very good, no matter how badly they were written, so it was an obvious place to make money writing.

But Eric Whelpton was a highbrow at heart, and he disliked popular fiction of any kind. His favorite Dorothy Sayers book was her translation of *Tristan*, which made no money and went quickly out of print. Being more secure financially, he apparently did not see that Dorothy was sensibly turning her lively talents towards a writing field that she enjoyed, but which also offered real possibilities to anyone willing to work. Dorothy knew enough about mysteries to realize that they were not all potboilers—that the best, like Wilkie Collins' *The Moonstone* and E. C. Bentley's *Trent's Last Case*, which had just come out in 1912, were closely related to the mainstream of novels of manners. Now she studied all types with her usual scholarly thoroughness.

Dorothy and Whelpton worked together at Les Roches for about a year, he remaining unaware of her personal interest in him. When he left to go to Italy—possibly because the school owner's daughter wanted him to marry her and run the school—they remained friends. Occasionally they ran into one another in London, where he once met her husband and did not like him. Whelpton eventually became a reporter and a radio broadcaster, working for the national press and various magazines on travel and international affairs. Thus his career, as it developed, had a lot in common with Dorothy's.

After Eric left Les Roches, Dorothy stayed on and finished the year. Les Roches had given her time to write while earning a living, but she was not an enthusiastic traveler and living abroad did not appeal to her; so once again she returned home.

She came back in time to take part in a gigantic Oxford University celebration. In 1919 women's education had taken a giant step forward with the passage of what was called the "Women's Statute." The bill passed Parliament on May 11, 1919, and became law on July 22. With its passage, women could now be granted university degrees and become full members of the university community. For the first time too, women at Oxford were required to wear academic dress. When she heard the good news, Dorothy shouted for joy. Now she could become a real Bachelor of Arts and in fact, at the same time, a Master of Arts, or in the Latin, *Domina*.

The excitement at Oxford over the change was tremendous. The women students even had to hold style shows for the men before an official university statute was passed declaring that the women would wear gowns like the men but soft caps instead of stiff mortarboards. They could also be caught by the proctors and their "bulldog" assistants if they were out late or gownless.

Thanks to Miss Penrose at Somerville, more than 300 of its graduates had taken all the necessary examinations, fulfilled the residential requirements, and paid the fees needed for a university degree. Students at Oxford are granted the B.A. degree when they finish their studies; then after they have been "down" a certain length of time and paid some more fees, they are automatically granted their M.A. degree.

On the 14th of October in 1920, a warm, sunny day

when the gray walls of Oxford's gothic buildings were hung with crimson vines that matched the university's academic hoods, a large crowd gathered in the Sheldonian Theatre to watch the first women get university degrees. In the audience watch the first women get university degrees. Although there was little outward excitement, the atmosphere was charged with emotion.

A special ceremony was held before the actual degrees were given out. In it the vice-chancellor conferred M.A. degrees on the five principals of the women's colleges, so that they would be able to take academic precedence over their students. The five came in together through the wide south doors and bowed to the vice-chancellor, who then robed and capped them. Then they took their proper places on the platform with the other university officials. The male undergraduates received their degrees next, because the order was not changed for several more years to "ladies first." Finally, seven candidates chosen from each of the women's colleges, among them Dorothy herself and her friend Muriel Byrne, came in last.

During the ceremony which followed, Dorothy and the others first became entitled to wear (and actually put on and took off) three different sets of academics. First, they were given the proper undergraduate gown, which in Dorothy's case was the scholar's long gown. Next, they briefly wore the "rabbit-skins," as they were called, which meant they were now Bachelors of Art. And last, they were given the crimson hoods of Masters of Arts and called by the formal title *Domina*. They also became eligible to pay three sets of fees on that single day to become properly enrolled Senior Members of the university. Dorothy forgot to pay hers and as a result was never allowed to attend convocation, the gathering of the official governing body of the university. The many other Somerville graduates eligible for degrees received theirs in 1921, among them Charis Barnett Frankenburg, whose small son Peter had to be taken out for talking too loudly.

That night at Somerville College's triumphant dinner, a special toast was offered to Miss Penrose for her foresight in making sure that the college would have the largest number of degrees granted when this day dawned. Dorothy's old tutor, Miss Pope, was also congratulated on being appointed Taylorian Lecturer in Modern Languages for the university, the first woman so honored in its history. It was a Gaudy Night indeed.

The Cottages & Gate-house: Somerville College;

Courtesy of Somerville College

Courtesy of Somerville College

A Bay of the
Library
Somerville
College

Courtesy of Somerville College

From a class photo, Somerville College (moved to Oriel during the War), 1915. Dorothy Sayers is the first person on the left in the third row from the bottom. Muriel St. Clare Byrne is sixth from the left in the back row. Dorothy Rowe is also in the back row, third from the right, wearing a large white hat.

Dorothy L. Sayers as scholar.

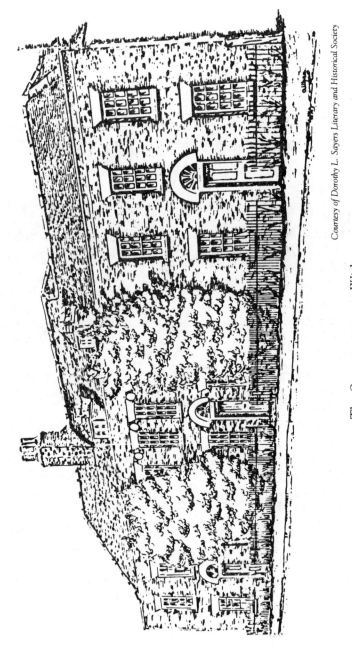

The Sayers cottage at Witham.

6

ADVERTISING AND THE
ARISTOCRACY

IN 1922, AFTER A SHORT SPELL TEACHING HIGH SCHOOL
in Clapham, Dorothy got a job as an advertising copywriter.
She went to work for a very successful London agency called
S. H. Benson's. It was located at Kingsway and Great Queen's
Street, in the heart of modern London, west of St. Paul's
Cathedral and the old city, and east of fashionable Mayfair
and Belgravia, which clustered about the parks near Bucking-
ham Palace.

S. H. Benson's was an established firm with a reputation
for creativity. Even before World War I, many of its copywriters had been university graduates who knew the classics,
quoted and wrote poetry, and could come up with witty slogans. Benson's had hired its first woman copywriter during the
war, and Dorothy now replaced her. When she started she was
paid four pounds a week, about twenty dollars, which was a
decent salary for a beginning job. Her father continued to give
her a small allowance to help pay the rent.

Copywriting involves writing the headlines and information about products which appear in advertisements. Educated, literary people who had no academic bent have often
found advertising a good career. It is amusing and clever work,
and once they learn the knack, they make good money.
Dorothy had always loved making up silly rhymes and jingles

and playing with words; she had a clear style of writing; and she found the slightly hectic atmosphere of an ad agency delightful after the prim formality and routines of teaching. She was also freer to do her own work in her own way, for as she pointed out,

> Everybody is always out of his room. If he isn't chatting with the copy-department, or fooling around the typists, he's in the studio, clamoring for a lay-out, or in the printing, complaining about a folder, or in the press-department, inquiring about an appropriation, or in the vouchers, demanding back numbers of something or if he isn't in any of those places, he's somewhere else—slipped out for surreptitious coffee or haircut.

The publishing techniques Dorothy had learned at Blackwell's were useful, because advertising also involved things like lettering and layouts and used printer's symbols. Dorothy was a good amateur artist and well able to sketch a layout to show how she wanted an ad to look. Oxford had trained her to have efficient, scholarly habits of thinking, as well as how to handle words and share information freely with others. This cooperative attitude made her pleasant to work with in an office which was in many ways not that different from a kind of community of scholars.

Dorothy turned out to be a natural copywriter. In her mystery *Murder Must Advertise*, in which she has Lord Peter pretend to be a copywriter to catch a murderer, she describes some of her own experiences. Like Benson's, "Pym's Publicity" had university people who clowned about, making up limericks and refusing to do any work until they had figured out the daily crossword puzzle. They were mixed in with more painstaking, hardworking types who were jealous of this giddy varsity crowd.

On Dorothy's first day, she, like Lord Peter, was dropped into this gay, noisy office by one of the top bosses, who told a fellow copywriter to start her on some product that the agency

I HOLD BY MY WHIMSY

Courtesy of Wilfred Scott-Giles

The Wimsey Coat of Arms, drawn by Wilfred Scott-Giles.

Sketch of Dorothy L. Sayers by John Gilroy R.A., 1930.

handled. When the boss went back to his private domain, she was sociably introduced to everybody from typists to errand boys and then taken to a tiny office with a table, a couple of chairs, and a battered desk where she was to work.

For her first lesson in copywriting, Dorothy was told to look through the scrapbooks of sample ads about her product and then try writing a few headlines herself. In her book she has Lord Peter write headlines for margarine, and some of those he comes up with, like "It is a far, far butter thing," sound exactly like her own clever slogans must have sounded.

Like Pym's, Benson's had special office teas and staff parties and played a yearly game of cricket against the team from an important client's staff. When there was a deadline or a client crisis of some kind, the whole agency became frantic, but with a sense of theater, the idea that the "show must go on," which made it hard work but fun. A secretary might suddenly appear with cups of a new instant cereal and make the copywriters all try some and describe it. When a very moral client came for a conference, everyone in the office had to quit smoking.

Dorothy worked at Benson's for nine years. A good copywriter made an excellent living because advertising was a booming industry, and she ended up one of the best paid in the trade. She is given credit for having invented the slogan, "It pays to advertise." She was also the chief copywriter for one of the most successful ad campaigns ever run in England. Benson's never had a more spectacular success than their campaign to help J. & J. Coleman sell more mustard. Benson's copy chief Oswald Green is given credit for the campaign idea, but it probably grew out of a typical agency brainstorming session with all the copywriters. At any rate, it was Dorothy who wrote most of the actual copy and made the Mustard Club go down in advertising history.

On Saturday, September 28, 1926, large posters began to appear in London's red buses with the headline, "Has Father joined the Mustard Club?" Next, there were coupons to send in to join, and letters and stories and cartoons in the newspapers. When the public was told what the ads were all about, their interest was kept by a series of tales about members of the Mustard Club, menus in restaurants, endorsements by famous movie stars, and kiddie contests to look the most like a mustard pot. The club was headed by its president, Baron de Beef, whose hobby was breeding Welsh Rabbits, and had members like Lord Bacon and Cookham, Lady Hearty and Miss DiGester. Some of the characters are supposed to have been based on people working at Benson's. The Mustard Club's success was nearly as great as Lord Peter's famous "Whiffle Around Britain" campaign which sold cigarettes from the cradle to the grave.

While she was becoming a copywriter, Dorothy was also enjoying life in London. She had an apartment at 24 Great James Street in Bloomsbury, which was within walking distance of her job. She in fact used this apartment in Great James Street as the model for Lord Peter's detective friend Charles Parker's flat at 12A Great Ormond Street just a few blocks away. Bloomsbury was a part of London where many young university graduates had lived since before the war. It had tall old townhouses built in the 18th century around garden squares, now cut up and turned into rooming houses and flats. Like Chelsea along the Thames River west of Parliament, this was a place where the young intellectuals lived and worked and talked about art and love and politics. The famous pre-war Bloomsbury Group, which included the writer Virginia Woolf, her husband, and her sister and brother-in-law Vanessa and Clive Bell, was very "Left," or Socialist, but its interest in theater and the arts had given the whole community a university atmosphere. Bloomsbury supported the idea of women's rights; it also had the reputation of being a place where couples lived together unmarried or had various affairs.

Although Dorothy had a number of good friends in London, such as Muriel Byrne and Marjorie Barber, her social life had its problems. Clever and amusing as she was, she was also tall and plain, and unlike her friends, she was not particularly sought out by men she considered eligible. It is likely that Dorothy had one or more casual affairs during the early 20s after she arrived in London, but none proved lasting nor seems to have been "great fun." Dorothy did not make her private life public then or later. The general public was still very Victorian in its outlook, as were the laws of the land. But she did not invent her knowledge of the problems caused by the habits and morals of her own generation; she wrote from her own observation and some personal experience.

Dorothy also developed a series of hobbies which she ruthlessly pushed on everyone about her until her own interest or money ran out. Many of these hobbies appear in her stories, among them crossword puzzles, photography, and riding a motorcycle. She bought herself a motorcycle and rode it home to Christchurch to visit her parents. She also quit playing the violin in favor of a saxophone to play jazz. As always when Dorothy got interested in something, she attacked it like a scholar, learning as much as she could about it. This is one of the reasons why her books are full of authentic details about so many different things.

All over Bloomsbury and Chelsea were hundreds of clubs representing all kinds of artistic and political interests. In her novels about the 20's Dorothy described several of them with an exaggerated, but realistic sense of humor:

> They stumbled up a narrow and encumbered stair, at the top of which a fine confused noise of a piano, strings, and the clashing of kitchen utensils announced that some sort of entertainment was in progress . . . hammered loudly on a door, and without waiting for an answer, flung it open . . . [to be] struck in the face . . . by a thick muffling wave of heat, sound, smoke and the smell of frying. It was a very small room, dimly lit by a single electric bulb, smothered in a lantern of painted glass, and it was packed

to suffocation with people, whose . . . pallid faces looked like glow-worms. . . . Ceiling wreaths of tobacco-smoke swam slowly to and fro in the mist.

The music being performed was composed by an artist named Stanislaus, whose new work on the Piccadilly tube (subway) station kept him traveling on the escalator five days to absorb the tone values.

Dorothy also found many of the political clubs amusing, particularly those with a Socialistic or Labor background because, both as a Christian and as a political Conservative, she did not agree with Socialism's basic understanding of mankind. To her an idea was not wrong just because it was also historic or traditional; on the contrary neither her experience nor her beliefs inclined her to take stock in the idea of Progress. In her short story "The Fascinating Problem of Uncle Mealeager's Will," she poked fun at both the Reds and the archconservative Primrose League.

With her love of music and drama Dorothy also took advantage of the cheap seats available in the hundreds of London theaters and concert halls. Her wide taste, like Lord Peter's, ran from organ recitals to vaudeville at the Palladium to clever romantic comedies to Shakespeare and his peers. Typically, too, she liked to poke fun at the modern theatrical productions which ignored plot or character development. One of her perenially favorite hobbies was a lively argument, a habit for which she was as well known at work as among her friends and acquaintances.

Bloomsbury is near Soho, the home of most of London's good foreign restaurants, and Dorothy and her friends quickly learned that they could find at her favorite places—like the Moulin d'Or on Romilly Street—the privacy people seek in genteel tea shops and never find. At first she had to put up with whatever her landlady fed her and live cheaply, but gradually, as she became better paid and able to afford good food and wine, she began to gain weight. She lost her lean look to become a stout, tailored businesswoman in suits and mannish hats.

While she was learning to live in London, Dorothy became a published novelist for the first time. *Whose Body?*, her first Lord Peter mystery, came out in 1923, when she was thirty. Her plot and characters, as her friend Barbara Reynolds has pointed out, echo in a number of respects E. C. Bentley's *Trent's Last Case*. She admired Bentley's book very much because it included real people and situations inside a puzzle plot. Both books have a murderer who "lives" his victim's life for a night to escape suspicion and the same basic motive for the murder itself. *Whose Body?* and possibly her second novel, *Clouds of Witness*, which is full of romantic adventures, may have been written before she came to London. But like most beginning authors, she needed several years to find a publisher. *Whose Body?*, in fact, was first published in America.

Until after the war, crime and detective stories had nearly all been written by men. Mystery writing was not yet a woman's field, with people like Agatha Christie, Margery Allingham, or Ngaio Marsh all producing series about detectives, as shortly began to happen. Dorothy herself was one of the first to be successful at the trade, partly because she had really studied the field and partly because she enjoyed mysteries herself. She became not only a writer of mysteries that people who did not like mysteries read, but also an authority on detective fiction.

Dorothy explained that when she put together a detective story, the idea usually came in a flash, perhaps from a conversation or a curious case in the newspaper. Then for a few days she went about in a happy glow of murderous enthusiasm, until she realized that she still had to sit down and do a lot of solid thinking to make up a plot. To her the real craft of writing is the work of telling the story.

Dorothy saw that all novelists consciously or unconsciously create their own worlds, which they make realistic by using particular details like street numbers and odd habits. Sherlock Holmes lives at 221 B Baker Street and is addicted to cocaine. From the beginning in her first book, Dorothy was writing about the Christian world, in which man is a fallen creature but able to choose between good and evil in a place where such choices matter. She saw mysteries as related to the long line of epic literature described by her mentor G. K. Chesterton as stories about St. George (the detective) slaying the dragon. At the same time she tried to rejoin detective stories to the mainstream of English literature, where motivation tried to be psychologically sound, and the villains were not all black and the heroes made of gold.

Her first great act of craftsmanship, which is still one of her chief claims to fame, was her creation of the unforgettable Lord Peter Wimsey himself. Lord Peter is "fair and Mayfair," a Wodehouse Bertie Wooster in horn-rims, a slim, rabbity fellow with a monocle, a beak of a nose, and handsome hands. He is jumpy and rattles on amusingly with a lot of mannerisms, quotes poetry by the yard, and has a valet, Bunter, who is superior to Jeeves in personality and poise. In his first appearance, however, Lord Peter is also a veteran who suffers from shellshock and nerves as a result of his wartime responsibilities, making him more a romantic hero than a cool oddity like Sherlock Holmes or a bundle of artificial mannerisms like Hercule Poirot. The older Lord Peter grew, the less superhuman he became, and the more complicated personality traits his creator revealed. But he was carefully crafted from the first to intrigue his readers.

Dorothy used background she knew to create Lord Peter's basic family history. She located the Wimseys in Norfolk and gave them the title of Denver, a village not far from Christchurch. She may have modeled the Wimseys originally on the one family in Eastern England whose name has been heard in English history since Bosworth Field in 1485, the Howards, dukes of Norfolk. Over the years she and her friend Wilfred Scott-Giles "discovered" a lot more Wimsey family history for

their own amusement, carefully making each detail historically accurate. She had thoughtfully made the Wimseys rich
not from land but from real estate and industrial development,
so that, unlike many of the postwar aristocracy, they still had
enough money to provide for a younger son.

There has been a lot of guessing about the origins of Lord
Peter. In 1936 Dorothy herself wrote an amusing, tongue-in-
cheek account of how she happened to create her character,
claiming that while she was thinking about writing a detective
story, he simply walked in and applied for the job. Lord Peter's
witty talk, his apt quotations and rhyming puns, his sharp
intelligence and fondness for puzzles and plots, as well as for
good food and drink, and his Elephant's Child curiosity, do
not need that much explanation: they are Dorothy's own.
Lord Peter is in many respects the man she might have been.
The notion that he was modeled upon Eric Whelpton or any
other man with whom Dorothy was in love is also far less
likely than that she simply studied the heroes of past literature
and created one to suit her purposes. But Lord Peter also has
the restlessness and depression of the postwar generation
Dorothy knew, making him even at birth one of the more
complicated detectives in mystery fiction.

Whose Body? was not a best-seller, but it did well enough
for Ernest Benn, its English publisher, to agree to publish
Dorothy's second mystery, *Clouds of Witness*. She was already
working on another when it came out in 1926. One very
useful thing about a job like writing copy was that she could
shut herself into her tiny office and claim to be working.
Then, if she really had no rush copy to produce, she could
work on another novel.

7

PRIVATE LIVES

JUST AS HER CAREER WAS WELL UNDER WAY, DOROTHY
faced a serious personal crisis. Biographical sketches published during her lifetime mentioned that she and her husband had an adopted son whose name was John Anthony
Fleming. At her death her public learned a little more about
him because he was her sole heir, apart from her old friend and
literary executor Muriel St. Clare Byrne, who received a small
bequest. Dorothy and her husband had unofficially adopted
Anthony when he was about ten, at the time he was sent to
boarding school. At her death he was a thirty-four-year-old
economist, just married, and living in London. The English
newspapers made a great fuss about his "sudden wealth," but
he pointed out in a manner very like his mother's that she had
not actually left him 35,000 pounds (about $100,000). That
was only the theoretical value which the government had
placed upon the future earnings of her books, whose copyright
he now owned.

But it was not until 1975 that it was disclosed in a book
about Dorothy by Janet Hitchman that John Anthony Fleming is Dorothy's own son, born out of wedlock in 1924, when
she was thirty. Probably Dorothy did not set out deliberately to have an illegitimate child because she did not acknowledge him openly and raise him herself alone. The post-war

72

period had made such situations commoner, but even Virginia Woolf's sister Vanessa, who had a daughter by her lover, raised her as her husband's child so that she could use his name and avoid the other legal complications of illegitimate children.

Society in general still had heavy penalties, legal and social, against unwed mothers. It was only in 1925 that *married* women were able to be legal guardians of their own children, while in 1927 the Legitimacy Act made a child legitimate if his parents afterwards married each other. In 1924 a mother and illegitimate child could acknowledge one another openly only if they did not care what anyone else thought of them, or care if their family were placed in a very difficult position. Under these circumstances it is not surprising that she objected to her private life being treated as "good copy." Dorothy undertook to live her entire adult life knowing that at any moment she might suddenly find herself, as her character Harriet Vane actually does, before the bar of public opinion, with the press having a field day discussing her morals in print.

When she found she was pregnant, Dorothy dealt with the situation with her customary vigor. There is no evidence that she had help apart from that of her family, particularly her cousin Ivy, who was the only one who knew all about the situation. The child was hers, and she not only wanted him, she felt responsible for him. She did not have an abortion, nor did she put him up for adoption. Instead, she arranged to take an eight-weeks leave of absence from Benson's so that she could finish *Clouds of Witness*, and went home to the Fens.

Her greatest immediate problem then and later was money, because she apparently felt that supporting her son was her job alone. From then on Dorothy became a kind of human dynamo, working hard at a fulltime job and still writing an incredible amount of other things free lance. As a career-oriented person, she tackled her problem in a "masculine" way, working hard to become a better source of support for herself and her expected child. Although her earlier books might have brought enough money to allow her to quit Benson's to write fulltime, they probably did not make enough for her to quit and support her son and pay for his education.

Whether or not she told her parents, Dorothy managed to keep her pregnancy a secret from her friends and business colleagues. She arranged to have the baby in a nursing home in Bournemouth and spent Christmas there. Anthony was born on January 3, 1924, and registered as her son, using her maiden name, in the district of Christchurch. In February Dorothy returned alone to London to work.

Her solution for taking care of Anthony while he was small was not particularly unusual at the time. Ivy Shrimpton was a foster mother who raised children for other people. Ivy now rented Cocksparrow Hall from the local squire in Westcott Barten, near Oxford. It was an old stone house a little way out of the village with no indoor plumbing or electricity. Miss Shrimpton came to live there with several children, one of whom was Anthony, and she is remembered in the village as very eccentric. She never went out shopping without strapping her purse to her wrist, and she let the garden and grounds about the house become a veritable jungle.

Dorothy had to contribute to this establishment, and she did. She came to visit, supposedly to see her cousin, and was seen leaving in tears. But it would have been nearly impossible for her to have kept Anthony in London with her, even with a fulltime nurse, and done the amount of writing she did in the next ten years.

Much has been said of Dorothy's public remarks about not liking children. But like so many comments Dorothy made, her statements about children need to be taken a little less seriously. One of the best ways to hide the fact that one has a child of one's own is to go on record against children, and it is a method that would have appealed to her sense of humor. As in many other instances, she probably protested too much. She got along well with the children of her friends, some of whom, like Charis Frankenburg's daughter, visited her when they were at school nearby. Her short stories about the Wimsey children show sensible but ironic views on modern childhood theories.

In her comedy called "Love All," about a novelist who deserts his wife and small son to run off with an actress, only to discover that his wife has written a smash hit play and has no desire to go back to him and his ego, Dorothy made some acid comments about parental responsibilities. Her heroine refuses to accept the idea that a boy must have his mother nearby while his father can skip the country or stay in London ignoring him. The whole play is a witty declaration of a woman's right to get as much emotional support from her marriage as a man traditionally expects from his. The small son ends up living in London with his grandmother so that his mother can go on writing plays and still see him every day.

Two years after Anthony's birth, in 1926, when she was thirty-four, Dorothy married Oswald Arthur Fleming, a divorced man who was twelve years older than she. He wrote and worked under the more romantic name of Atherton Fleming, which she also used as her married name. But she followed the typical postwar pattern of using her maiden name professionally. She may have met Fleming through her work in advertising and he may have actually worked at Benson's with her.

"Mac," as he was called, was Scottish, the son of a customs official who was working in the Orkney Islands when he was born. He had four brothers and a sister. Two of his brothers were killed in the First World War and a third was badly wounded, while Mac himself seems to have undergone experiences in the trenches that changed his entire life. Dorothy's characters Lord Peter and George Fentiman owe some of their wartime "scars" to Mac, particularly Fentiman, who cannot keep a steady job, has terrible fits of depression, and even loses his mind periodically when life is too much for him. He is also abusive to his wife, who has to support them both. A similar situation existed in the Fleming household, particularly in the later years when he did little but drink at the local pub, but he was also proud of her and once said she was sure to be made a Dame.

Mac did not come from the same social class as someone like Eric Whelpton, nor did he go to a university. Before the war he had married the daughter of an ordained minister who ran a small prep school, and they had two daughters. Mac had worked in Coventry, doing advertising and promotional work for Daimlers, the famous English automobile company, as well as other work on the side. He was a skilled photographer and a good amateur painter.

When the war broke out, he served for a time as a special correspondent for the *Daily Chronicle,* then volunteered and ended up as a captain in the Army Service Corps. In 1919 he published a book called *How to See the Battlefields*. As he says in the foreword, he was not writing a history of the war but trying to help people who wanted to see where the fighting had been or visit the graves of their family or friends. He included in the book some brief experiences of his own, together with a number of maps and diagrams of battle areas and suggestions as to people one might ask for help. Apart from this book, little is known about his wartime experiences, but he liked to tell tall tales about serving in the Foreign Legion under an assumed name. To the embarrassment of Dorothy's more proper friends, he also assumed the rank of "Major" and was known by it after the war. He seems to have had a strong streak of spoofing and showing off, not unlike Dorothy on occasion, but he was also considered a brilliant storyteller and she probably enjoyed listening to him herself.

A description of Mac about the time of the First World War makes it clear that he was a very attractive person with typically English good looks. He was nearly six feet tall, with bright brown hair and light blue eyes, slim, with broad shoulders and a long, straight nose and a military moustache. He had a husky, appealing voice and an irresistible grin that made his eyes light up. In many ways he and Dorothy were the same kind of people—humorous, dramatic, and in good moods, full of spirits. Mac and Eric Whelpton and Dorothy's son Anthony were all the same physical type, so that at various times gossip has said that one of them was Anthony's father, although neither is, according to information in Dorothy's private papers.

No one seems to know whether Mac worked steadily after the war. He had been an excellent copywriter and produced short stories too, but his personal problems, which began with the war, kept him from participating much in Dorothy's professional or social life. His first wife, to whom he simply never returned after the war, finally divorced him in 1925.

His divorce made it impossible for him and Dorothy to be married in church. Even so, her parents seem to have accepted him, although they apparently had hardly heard of him before the marriage. There is little doubt that Dorothy eventually supported both of them. Mac suffered more and more from depression, which made him unable to work. But in the 1930s the Bodley Head published a cookbook of his called *The Gourmet's Book of Food and Drink*, which he dedicated to his wife, "who can make an omelette." He also published a book on short story writing under a pen name. Her notebooks show that she and he discussed writing and things related to their professional lives. The more successful she became, however, the more difficult their life together must have been.

Still, Dorothy was protective of Mac to the point of being savage with his first family, for when his daughters tried to get in touch with him, she refused to allow them to upset him in person or by letter. No one knows how much her behavior came from jealousy of his first family and how much from a need to keep him emotionally quiet.

Her son's existence also created an unresolved conflict in her marriage. Mac knew about him, since when Anthony was old enough to go to prep school he used the name of John Anthony Fleming and Mac was listed there and in the Oxford University records as his father. Dorothy's marriage did provide Anthony with a convincing enough background to keep him from being talked about, although there was always some speculation as to whether or not he was really Mac's son.

The newly married couple lived in Dorothy's apartment in Great James Street. By 1928 they had taken over more room there, and in a letter Dorothy described the confusion of redecorating with the carpets up, the painters painting, the cat poking in the cracks and corners, and Mac pretending to be the town officials of Ypres, out inspecting the damage after a bombing. She herself felt more like Dido trying to build Carthage.

Dorothy bought an inexpensive car to replace the motorcycle which she kept for pleasure jaunts, and Mac kept the car in working order. It was not at all like Lord Peter's "Mrs. Merdle," but since Mac had worked for Daimlers, he was a source of information on these and other expensive cars as well. Dorothy used the car to visit her parents and her small son.

Still working at Benson's, writing mysteries, and keeping house for herself and Mac, Dorothy often complained loudly about servants who departed and left her to cope with her own cooking and cleaning. For the most part, however, she really seems to have found quite good help one way or the other. Like most husbands—even those married to career women—Mac did not contribute much to running the house except to take phone messages, which he often lost. No wonder Dorothy wrote up an idyllic situation in *Busman's Honeymoon* in which Harriet is free of household worries because Lord Peter has loftily informed *his* mother that she must get a housekeeper so that his wife's writing time will not be interrupted by uproars in the servants' hall. But in the unfinished sequel, *Thrones, Dominations*, Dorothy portrays Harriet less grandly as having to cope with servants' crises and the other interruptions of married life.

MAKER AND CRAFTSMAN

In October 1928, when her father died, leaving an estate of 5000 pounds, Dorothy bought a cottage for her mother and Aunt Leigh and the parrot to live in together. The cottage was called "Sunnyside," and it was in Witham, Essex, a quiet little market town on the London Road, with good train connections to the city. After the death of Mrs. Sayers in 1929, Aunt Leigh went on living there and Dorothy and Mac began to use the cottage themselves as a weekend house.

The appearance in Witham of a writer of detective stories was a kind of nine days' wonder at first, but since Dorothy came to Witham to find a quiet place to work undisturbed, she became acquainted in the town very slowly. She was therefore thought rather snobbish and unsociable by the people who felt that they ought to be meeting her socially, although the tradespeople with whom she dealt seem to have liked her from the start. But she ordered much of what she used from London, and until the Second World War also spent more time there.

In 1930 she bought the cottage next door, Number 22, and remodeled the two cottages into one. They had been built in the 15th century, right on the main road, but had been given false fronts to look like 18th-century townhouses. They had neat, regular windows, and tall chimneys, and gardens in back. Each cottage had two storeys and an attic. The floorplans were slightly different, and bathrooms and toilets had been stuck into closets and turns of the stairs. Many of the rooms had fireplaces, but each cottage had a regular boiler room in the basement as well. Witham was probably the inspiration for Talboys, the Wimseys' country cottage, although physically the two places were not much alike.

8

SUCCESS

Despite the complications in her private life, Dorothy had become by thirty-five the person she was to remain. She was a popular, successful writer with a growing public. Since she was very busy, she was easily annoyed by interruptions or demands upon her precious time. Always the uncompromising perfectionist who expected the most of herself and everybody about her, she got herself into trouble with the press, her publishers, and her public. She was working at a man's job and demanded equal rights, but she often had to fight to get them. Her friends, fortunately, were better acquainted with the sense of humor that was her saving grace; they also knew that like many writers she was really rather shy.

Behavior that made Dorothy seem odd or difficult is really typical of artists. Writing requires long hours of concentration. It is not a trade like mopping floors that can be done whether or not the brain is working full speed ahead. A thought broken off in midstream may take days to reappear, if it ever does. Moreover, the discipline of writing requires that the writer work at his or her craft daily.

Until 1931 Dorothy was still working fulltime in advertising. She was also producing at least one mystery novel a year about Lord Peter Wimsey, as well as short stories about him.

In addition, she joined and helped to found several literary clubs, gave speeches and wrote articles, and kept up a huge correspondence. In 1920, while working on her translation of the story of Tristan and Isolde, she had joined the Modern Language Association. Parts of her *Tristan* were published in the MLA's magazine *Modern Languages*, and in 1930 she became its president.

In her correspondence with friends and fans—which she wrote out in her clear, handsome longhand—she often thought aloud. She worked out plots, discussed the public's wishes and rights, fussed about details, and complained about having too much to do. Like her lectures and articles, her letters sound conversational, unmistakably echoing her manner of talking. They are usually amusing as well.

To her public, as she grew stouter (after the custom of many mystery writers, among them Mrs. Christie and Miss Allingham), Dorothy appeared to be a jolly human dynamo. She was often drawn in cartoons with a grin on her face and a Sherlock Holmes cap on her head. But both the public and press still acted as if she were a more mysterious writer than she really was. She did not switch from one kind of writing to another abruptly, but instead kept her hand in on various kinds of writing all her working life. Some of her Oxford friends were surprised that she wrote detective stories after a university career of composing long, intellectual poems, though she never quit working on translations, some of which appeared only as elaborately illustrated Christmas cards to her friends (a number of them were joint projects with Mac). But it was not until some point during the Second World War, when she became totally absorbed in translating Dante, that she stopped writing about Lord Peter. She needed money and she had to keep writing what earned her the most until she finally could live off the royalties of her books and plays and suit herself.

Most of the time she now wore a recognizable costume which was sensible if not very glamorous. Usually she had her dark hair combed back and cut short. It grew thinner as she got older, and to hide it she took to wearing hats that pulled down about her ears. Year round she wore expensively tailored suits of different materials (but not tweeds), and she smoked cigarettes in a long holder. She usually had a pair of steel-rimmed or rimless glasses perched on her nose, which hid the dark, level eyebrows so noticeable in her earlier photographs. But when she dressed to go out to a party, she wore long handsome gowns and dangling earrings and once appeared with a ring on every finger and thumb. She looked to be what she was by birth and background—a member of English "County" society. She would have been quite ordinary among people who rode to the hounds, but she seemed eccentric in London's artistic community.

In 1927 her third mystery came out. It introduced the world to Miss Climpson, her emphatic, bracelet-jangling Edwardian spinster, and its plot hinged upon women's relationships with one another, as well as on a missing heir who was discovered by tracking down the family at Somerset House, a place in London where all births are recorded. The book was called *Unnatural Death* in England, *The Dawson Pedigree* in America. Some people think Miss Climpson is modeled upon Dorothy's cousin Ivy Shrimpton, who was taking care of her son; Dorothy did have a habit of "borrowing" names for characters by changing them only a little. The first of her country clergymen, Mr. Tredgold, also appeared in the story, so her father was able to read about him before he died.

In 1927 Dorothy had joined the Society of Authors, where she promptly became known as an outspoken defender of both mystery writers and women writers. She protested about a very distinguished reviewer who gave away the plots of every mystery he did not like and who panned anything written by women on principle. Since she was not the only writer to suffer from this man, she was not so much defending herself as working for the cause of equal rights and fair play.

The following year Dorothy produced so many things at

once that she must have been in perpetual motion. First, her fourth Lord Peter story, *The Unpleasantness at the Bellona Club*, a club of retired "warriors," was published by her new publisher, Victor Gollancz. Mr. Gollancz had been a bright, aggressive young editor at Benn's with whom Dorothy got along well. When he left to start his own firm in 1926, he took Dorothy with him. The switch created problems, since Benn had already printed *Unnatural Death* and had options on her next two books, but by 1928 the matter had been settled and Gollancz put out all the rest of her books, with a few exceptions during the war and the Dante translations.

They do not seem to have had rows over money, but occasionally Dorothy got angry at Gollancz because of his aggressive advertising methods. To sell *The Nine Tailors*, for example, he dreamed up the idea of announcing that it was *not* true that 100,000 people had bought her last book. A lot of the press was fooled into running stories saying the book *had* sold that many copies.

Still, he was very helpful. He got rid of the pests who complained she had used their name or written up their great aunts, and she wrote him long letters about each book as she was working on it. She told him about the problems of getting technical information on bell-ringing, or her annoyance at reviewers who were critical when the murderer could be picked out early in the book. She personally liked mysteries in which the reader could guess quickly who had done it but had to figure out how. She was irritated by readers who wanted love interest and equally irritated by readers who were angry when Lord Peter fell in love with Harriet Vane. Perhaps her loudest cries were kept for any miserable mortal who forgot that she was Dorothy L. Sayers! She said she never saw mention of "George Shaw."

Her books were one of the Gollancz firm's main assets. He later published her religious plays and essays, while still hoping she would write another Lord Peter book. But it took a while before he allowed Penguin to put out Lord Peter in their famous greenbacked series of best mysteries. When they did, Dorothy and Agatha Christie were the only writers to have two mysteries each in the original list. Dorothy's books stayed in print in hardcover too, and sold well in a variety of editions.

Next, still during 1928, Dorothy wrote an introduction to an anthology of famous short mystery stories which she personally selected, using her wide knowledge of the field. The anthology was called *Great Short Stories of Detection, Mystery and Horror,* although when it came out in America it was *The Omnibus of Crime.* Many experts still consider her introduction to be the finest single piece of writing about the detective story that was ever published, and it is still reprinted. She eventually went on to edit two other mystery anthologies for Gollancz.

A characteristic that appears over and over again in her writing is that she did not separate literature into different categories. Whatever she was reading—and she read everything she could get her hands on—she then compared to all the other things she had read. Given her scholarly background, she simply could not resist translating an idea from one story to another, or fail to see similarities in very different kinds of work. In her introduction to the crime stories, for example, Dorothy comments that a method used to catch Tristan in Isolde's bedroom (sprinkling flour on the floor so their footprints show) is an old detective trick.

She also pointed out that the modern detective story in which policemen are the heroes could not have been written until there was a good police organization and a public that respected it. In England that happened in the middle of the 19th century when Sir Robert Peel started his "Bobbies," with Scotland Yard as their headquarters. She also reminded her readers that the world's unexplored horizons had disappeared by then, so the only wild beast left to hunt was the murderer. She saw the modern detective as the true heir of epic superheroes like Roland and King Arthur, who protected the weak against the strong.

Finally, still in 1928, a collection of Dorothy's short stories called *Lord Peter Views the Body* came out. Most of these stories had first appeared in magazines like *Nash's* or *Grant Magazine* or *Ellery Queen*, some the kind to which Harriet Vane admits selling stories in order to buy Lord Peter a wedding gift. A number of these stories have been reprinted in various other anthologies as well. Some are bits and pieces of Lord Peter's "biography," a few are real horror stories, and some are more comedies of manners than true mysteries. Their whimsical titles often sound like G. K. Chesterton's, as in *The Incredible Elopement of Lord Peter Wimsey*.

In 1929, when she had proved she could write successfully, her first publisher, Benn, consented to put out Dorothy's translation of a 12th-century version of the story of Tristan. It was a very literary book, the kind a don might have published to enhance his academic reputation. It brought her very little money and was soon out of print. When she mentioned it long afterwards, she commented wryly that it had shown her she must "abandon verse translation and produce something that would earn its keep and mine." Still, she was bothered at "leaving behind me so many castles that I assaulted... and was obliged to abandon unreduced... these things still trouble me from time to time—in bed, or in the bath." Her state of mind is reflected on *Tristan's* title page, where her full name appears—as if to say, "this is the real Dorothy Leigh Sayers."

The translation itself is simple and straightforward. In it Dorothy tried to make the poem clear and interesting to a modern reader, because, as she claimed, the story of Tristan is a thoroughly "modern" story about morality and motives. It is a "frank exposure of the squalid accompaniments of unlawful love." She not only dedicated the book to Miss Pope, but thanked her for having gone over the text for errors, showing that she had kept in touch with Oxford while working hard in London.

Dorothy also found time to have fun. When the mystery writer Anthony Berkeley founded the Detection Club in 1928, Dorothy lent a hand. The club met every few months or so for a dinner and discussion, and they eventually rented some club rooms at 31 Gerrard Street, which is also the site of her "Soviet Club." Its first president was G. K. Chesterton, who continued to be the "ruler" until he died in 1936. Then E. C. Bentley, who wrote *Trent's Last Case,* as well as a very amusing parody of a Lord Peter mystery which he entitled *Greedy Night,* took over until 1949. Dorothy herself then became president until her death, when Agatha Christie succeeded her. The club's first secretary was John Dickson Carr.

Membership in the Detection Club was kept small, and election to membership was a sign of professional recognition. The club paid the rent for its rooms and criminological library with royalties from three detective novels in which the members collaborated. Dorothy participated in all three. The first one was called *The Floating Admiral,* which was published in 1931 and had fourteen collaborators, including G. K. Chesterton, Agatha Christie, and Ronald Knox. It is about a very dead admiral of the British Navy. Each member wrote a chapter, following notes and clues left him or her by the previous writer, and in some cases using each other's detectives as well. The second novel was called *Ask A Policeman,* which Helen Simpson worked on, and the third, *Double Death.*

Dorothy was in her element in the club. She helped to develop the elaborate initiation rite used at the formal yearly dinner held in a London restaurant such as the Cafe Royal. She probably wrote, or helped to write, the Detective Club's Oath of Membership, which is very funny but imposes the serious professional standards that Dorothy insisted upon in her work. The candidate stands before the President, hand upon a skull with a lighted candle inside (the skull known affectionately as "Eric"), and makes a series of promises which sound like a parody of the Orders of Baptism and Matrimony from the *Book of Common Prayer.* The President asks:

> Do you promise that your Detectives shall well and truly detect the Crimes presented to them, using those Wits

which it shall please you to bestow upon them, and not placing reliance upon, nor making use of, Divine Revelation, Feminine Intuition, Mumbo-Jumbo, Jiggery-Pokery, Coincidence, or the Act of God!

And the candidate must answer, "I do."

In 1930 Dorothy published *Strong Poison* and *The Documents in the Case*. Both of them were departures from the past. In *Strong Poison* she did the sort of thing she had said would destroy a detective story unless it was absolutely vital to the plot: she introduced Harriet Vane and let Lord Peter fall in love with her. Since Harriet is on trial for murder, her presence is certainly necessary to the plot, but some of Dorothy's readers protested violently just the same.

Most of them, however, fell for Harriet, whose shy, abrupt, humorous personality with its bright intelligence typified for them the educated modern woman. From that point on, many of Dorothy's readers divided themselves into two camps: those who grew increasingly interested in Harriet—so much so that they felt she threw herself away on Lord Peter—and those who resented Harriet's existence and often accused Dorothy of falling in love with Peter herself.

Dorothy disliked the sloppy habit of identifying a character with the author or trying to "excavate the author's personality and opinions from his books . . . because these efforts are an assault upon the independence of his creatures." Like most of her public protests, however, the reader must take this assertion with caution, for there is much of the world of Dorothy L. Sayers in the world of Harriet and Peter Wimsey.

Dorothy also had strong convictions about the integrity of literary characters, as is beautifully illustrated in *Strong Poison*. From its compelling opening scene in court, with the dry-as-dust judge and the sulky prisoner at the bar, it is Dorothy at her dramatic best. But in 1928, recent enough for us to be certain that Dorothy had read it, her new friend

Helen Simpson had collaborated with Clemence Dane on a mystery called *Enter Sir John*. Sir John is a brilliant actor-producer in the London theater who is also an amateur hero-detective. He not only saves the young ingenue on trial for murder, but falls in love with her and marries her to live happily ever after. There are parallel scenes and situations in the two books, but Dorothy, in a realism not yet typical of mysteries, refuses to betray Harriet's essential character with a fairytale romance. *Strong Poison* seems to be a case of Dorothy saying blandly, "Here you are, my dears, this is the way you should have done it."

Her other 1930 book, *The Documents in the Case,* is the only book she ever wrote with a single collaborator. His name appeared as "Robert Eustace," but he was really Dr. Eustace Robert Barton, a medical doctor and a mystery writer as well. He often helped writers by supplying scientific or medical facts for their books. The basic plot of *The Documents in the Case* seems to have come from a real-life situation, the Bywater-Thompson case which had happened in 1923. The story is told in a series of letters and other documents, a technique several other authors Dorothy knew had used recently, and the solution to its murder hinges upon a problem of organic chemistry. One of its most interesting features is the series of comments on writing as a profession made by two of the characters, a struggling writer and his successfully published fiancee.

About this point in her career, her rising sales as well as her growing concern about the ethics of advertising, which she said taught people to need things they had never wanted and manipulated the so-called educated public far too much, led her to quit advertising. Beginning in 1931 she devoted herself fulltime to her writing and lecturing. While still at Benson's she had always had mixed feelings about advertising. She realized that it was the only way to move merchandise in large markets; at the same time she hated the fact that the public was taken in by claims that were vague, half-true, or otherwise misleading. Her attitude was later expressed humorously and sardonically in a paragraph from *Murder Must Advertise:*

> All over London the lights flickered in and out, calling on the public to save its body and purse; Sopo Saves Scrubbing—Nutrax for Nerves. . . . It isn't Dear, It's Darling. . . . The presses, thundering and growling, ground out the same appeals by the million: Ask your Grocer, Ask Your Doctor, Ask the Man Who's Tried It. . . . Whatever you're doing, stop it and do something different! . . . Never Let Up. Never go to sleep! Never be Satisfied!

Between 1931 and about 1935, having finished her *Tristan* translation and seen it into print, Dorothy began another major academic work. She started a full-scale critical study of Wilkie Collins, the mystery writer and novelist of the 19th century whose *Moonstone* she much admired. About a quarter of the projected work was actually written before she became too involved with other things, but in letters she kept looking back at it, wishing she had time to complete it.

Before she left Benson's, Dorothy had also begun to write for yet another field—radio. In England the only radio network was the British Broadcasting Corporation, a nationally owned public institution. Its job was to provide the kind of public entertainment and information which public television channels put on today. Different programs were aimed at different areas and parts of the population. Today, the B.B.C. also runs two television networks and, incidentally, has produced several versions of Dorothy's mysteries.

The B.B.C. asked Dorothy to work on a collective, or "omnibus," detective story serial to be broadcast live. Five other mystery writers were involved: Agatha Christie, Ronald Knox, E. C. Bentley, Valentine Williams, and Hugh Walpole. Their first serial was broadcast in 1930 and called "Behind the Screen." Dorothy read her own episode aloud, and the B.B.C. then asked her to give some radio talks on her experiences as a writer. This was the beginning of a long, on-again, off-again relationship between Dorothy and the B.B.C. which is well documented in their files by hundreds of her letters.

Later that same year the B.B.C. asked Dorothy to be in charge of organizing another detective serial. She was offered a large fee to persuade Agatha Christie, Anthony Berkeley, E. C. Bentley, Freeman Croft Wills, and Clemence Dane—all Detection Club members—to help her. This serial was called "The Scoop," and like the first one was not a dramatized script calling for actors but was read aloud like a book. The point of this serial is that one daily newspaper gets a "scoop" over its rival. Dorothy wrote and broadcast the first segment, which ends with a typical Sayers sentence: "Rumbling and clanking in the pride of their fantastic circulation, two million *Morning Stars* sang together; they shouted for joy. They had their scoop after all."

Dorothy found working on these serials great fun and was disappointed that Agatha Christie was bored by it. Unlike Dorothy, Agatha would not stay around to argue about the production, but would quietly slip away. Dorothy did more programs and broadcasting over the next few years, then refused any more B.B.C. jobs after a row over leaving out her middle initial "L."

Her next Lord Peter mystery was *The Five Red Herrings*, which was published in 1931. It was written about an actual village, Kirkcudbright, which is in Galloway on the southwest coast of Scotland. The Scottish border country is famous as an artists' haunt because of its lovely heather-covered hills and gorgeous sunsets over the Irish Sea. Dorothy dedicated the book to the local landlord, "my friend Joe Dignam," adding, "Here at last is your book about Gatehouse and Kirkcudbright. All the places are real places and all the trains are real trains and all the landscapes are correct."

Before the Second World War Dorothy and Mac went there regularly in September on holiday, and stayed at No. 14

A in the High Street. Mac probably painted and fished because, as Dorothy said, everybody in Galloway did one or the other and if they did neither they were considered odd. Although she loved the countryside and the people, Dorothy spent most of her time writing. The local inhabitants remember her because she wore outlandish outfits like an old-fashioned country clergyman, with thick stockings and heavy brogues (a kind of Scottish shoe), had a loud voice, and talked a lot. She also dearly loved the local delicacies—fish, potato scones, and gingercake.

The plot of *Five Red Herrings* is based upon train schedules. Dorothy meant the book to be a pure puzzle with six possible suspects to show her critics that she could write a mystery in which the reader had to work to guess who the murderer is. But for many of her readers the book is less entertaining than some of her others because it is so full of timetables and has less Wimsey. Finding a happy medium between a puzzle plot and a novel of manners was a difficult problem even for someone as gifted as Dorothy. Her next Lord Peter book, *Have His Carcase* (or *Habeas Corpus*), which came out in 1932, features a plot based on blood clotting and tides, as well as a continuation of Peter and Harriet's romance. The same year she began work on two more mysteries which are among her very best, *Murder Must Advertise* and *The Nine Tailors*.

She finished *Murder Must Advertise* first because she knew its background so well she had no research to do. She hoped that her readers would enjoy learning about advertising, and she probably hoped that she could make them more alert to the power of words. After her death the American advertising journal *Ad Age* remarked that *Murder Must Advertise* was the best advertising story ever written, both the most realistic and the most amusing.

The Nine Tailors appeared in 1934 and was a huge success. It was even chosen by the Book Society, which was unusual for a mere mystery, and is still many people's favorite.

It also made the subject of change-ringing popular, since bell-ringing is at the center of the plot. Dorothy was asked to give lectures on the subject, which she did with her usual gusto, dividing up the audience into groups and having them "act out" ringing a peal. Her name still comes up today in articles about bells, though critics have found fault with a few technical points in the novel. After the book was written, she was taken up in a bell tower at Croydon while the bells were being rung, and she did not care for the experience. But she was very pleased when the Essex Society of Change-Ringers made her a life member.

Gaudy Night, published late in 1935, was written during a period when Dorothy was being an active Oxford alumna. She had been elected chairman of the Association of Senior Members of Somerville and held the job for two years, making frequent trips to Oxford for meetings. As she became more of a celebrity, she was asked to speak at more and more places. Between 1933 and 1935 she wrote reviews of mysteries for the *London Sunday Times* and gave talks to groups as varied as the Forum Club and the Stationer's Guild. In March of 1935 she read a paper at Oxford on "Aristotle and Detective Fiction," which she gave again to the English Association in June. It was later printed in a book of her essays called *Unpopular Opinions.*

Like many of her talks it was perfectly serious and extremely funny at the same time, because, whether or not Aristotle's definition of tragedy fits the detective story, the very idea of using him as an authority on this form was a clever joke to an Oxford audience. Altogether typical of Dorothy, it was like the "Nonsense Game" which she and her friends liked to play. They wrote learned papers on Sherlock Holmes, deadpan serious, as if he were real and they were scholars bound to clarify important dates or theses about him.

In the case of Aristotle too, Dorothy was showing one of her most characteristic attitudes. She saw the similarities between statements, even when they seemed to be from different worlds. Because of her ability to relate Aristotle and detective fiction to each another, she broadened the outlook both of the Oxford graduate who read the classics and the man on the street who picked up her mysteries. To her, all books belonged to literature and to life.

Gaudy Night is a university novel, set in Oxford, and she used her own college of Somerville as a model for her fictional Shrewsbury College. Dorothy said that it was the only book she had ever written which had any kind of moral, and it was a moral about which she felt a crusader's zeal—the integrity of the mind as one of the great permanent values in an emotionally unstable world. In Dorothy's view places like Oxford exist to be havens of peace and mental stimulation in a dangerous world.

Dorothy gave the toast at the 1935 Gaudy when the college honored Miss Pope, who was leaving for Manchester. During this period she also was a guest speaker at the Oxford Union, where she spoke in support of the motion that "the present excessive indulgence in the solution of fictitious crime augurs ill for our national future."

While Dorothy was making a name for herself, her old college friends were very busy with their own careers. Those who lived outside London saw Dorothy only when they came to town or at college reunions. A member of the Mutual Admiration Society suggested that the initials now stood for Middle-Aged Spread.

Many of her friends were active in community affairs, serving on boards and promoting causes like birth control clinics and child care facilities. Charis Frankenburg, for example, was involved in Conservative politics and midwifery; she also was elected a Magistrate of the Juvenile Court of Salford and still found time to write a Latin primer for her four children which was published with saucy drawings by Dorothy Rowe. Unlike the primer Dorothy had learned from, this one has the whale (*balaena*) eat the sailors (*nauta*).

It was in London primarily that Dorothy moved within a circle of friends. Each worked at her own writing independently, but kept up with what the others were doing, giving aid and comfort when needed, and occasionally collaborating on projects for their mutual amusement. The group had in common the ability to quote any kind of literature, especially Shakespeare, often playing with it to entertain themselves. They also shared interests in education, the theater, and religion—and they all liked cats. Primarily, these were the people to whom she dedicated *Busman's Honeymoon*, saying,

> Dear Muriel, Helen and Bar,
>   With what extreme of womanly patience you listened to this tale . . . while it was being written, the Lord He Knoweth. I do not like to think how many times I tired the sun with talking—and if at any time they had told me you were dead, I should easily have believed that I had talked you into your graves. . . .

Helen Simpson originally came from Australia and was part French. She became a member of the Detection Club in 1931, and met Dorothy there. A devout Roman Catholic, she shared Dorothy's intellectual interest in theology and in education. Her husband, Dennis Brown, was a doctor, and they had one daughter. Helen was a marvellous addition to the Detection Club because she entered into its elaborate ceremonies with the proper gravity. She also helped the club spend the money it had made from its detective novels by furnishing their rooms from the second-hand store of one of her husband's patients. Helen not only wrote mysteries with Clemence Dane as her co-author, but she published other novels, including *Boomerang*, about her French and Australian ancestors. This novel, her last, won the James Tait Black prize for literature. She also wrote a popular biography of Henry VIII.

Muriel Byrne and Marjorie Barber were now living in a terraced house in St. John's Wood. After Muriel's mother died, they had rented the house to be near the South Hampstead High School for Girls, where Marjorie had continued to teach. Like the rest of their generation, they had a housekeeper and a cleaning woman, but Marjorie ran the household because she liked to cook. A portrait of Marjorie painted by Mac hangs in their living room. She was the only one of the group who did not consider herself a wit or a serious writer. But whenever she wanted to make some extra money, she sat down, wrote, and sold a short story to one of the popular women's magazines. She published them under the pen name "May Sinclair," which she had borrowed from Muriel.

Muriel St. Clare Byrne, who has been awarded the Order of the British Empire and is a Governor of the Royal Memorial Theatre of Stratford on Avon, also taught literature for a time at the South Hampstead High School. But finding that she disliked being tied down to one job, she also did research in the historical documents of the Tudor period and gave lectures for the Royal Drama Society. (She was the best Shakespearean of the group.) In 1922 she wrote a short history of Somerville College to help it raise money after the war, and in 1925 she published a study of Elizabethan town and country life. In 1936 she was the editor of a group of letters of Henry VIII which she not only selected but translated, where needed, out of French or Latin into modern English. Her introductions to these books are entertaining, informative, and full of quotations. In *Henry VIII* she thanks Marjorie for enduring the king's giant bulk and overwhelming personality about the house for two years and for reading the proofs; she thanks Dorothy for some help with linguistic problems in translation.

This group often met to dine and talk until late at night as if they were still students in college. Dorothy and Muriel never lost their undergraduate trick of staying up late to work, and their interests and enthusiasms rubbed off on one another. For their own amusement they wrote one another elaborate imitations of Elizabethan works, like the series of poems on the "Signs of the Zodiack" which Dorothy wrote Muriel one year. Dorothy even got her druggist to mix her up some Elizabethan ink (Muriel was an expert in dating manuscripts) and wrote the poems out herself in Elizabethan handwriting.

The group also amused themselves playing games with the Wimseys. After 1935 Dorothy began to add to Lord Peter's background by inventing his urbane old uncle Paul. He told about Peter's early love life in a new introduction which was added to later editions of all the mysteries. There was a letter to *The Times*, signed "Mathew Wimsey," which was about the Wimsey family chin, and in 1936 the whole group produced the "Papers relating to the Family of Wimsey."

This was a spoof pamphlet telling about the tenth duke of Denver, whose son and heir married beneath him in the late 18th century. Dorothy and Helen wrote most of the material in imitation 18th-century style, while two other friends, Mr. and Mrs. Scott-Giles, drew the large Wimsey Coat of Arms for the title page and the portrait of the grim-looking tenth duke for the frontispiece. Another friend, W. J. Redhead, who had "designed" Fenchurch St. Paul's for Dorothy's *The Nine Tailors*, made a drawing of the ancestral Wimsey home, Bredon Hall. Helen arranged to have the pamphlet printed privately by Humphrey Milford, but it was never reissued for the general public.

In March 1937 Dorothy, Muriel, Helen, and Scott-Giles all spoke on the Wimsey family to the Confraternitas Historica at Sidney Sussex College, Cambridge. Dorothy's paper was "An Account of Lord Mortimer Wimsey, the Hermit of the Wash," who was convinced that he was one of the fishes drawn up by St. Peter in the Miraculous Draught, so he lived in the sea like a fish and was known as "Old Scaley." She later sent it to her friends as a Christmas card.

The most diligent of the Wimsey historians was Wilfred Scott-Giles, an historian who also held the office of Fitzalan Pursuivant. In this capacity he served as a royal herald under the direction of the duke of Norfolk, who is in charge of ceremonial occasions, and was present at the state funeral of Sir Winston Churchill and at Caernarvon when Prince Charles was made Prince of Wales.

Scott-Giles had become acquainted with Dorothy in 1936 by writing her a letter. He asked her about the origins of the Wimsey coat of arms with its cat and three mice. She promptly wrote back to tell him that the arms were originally three silver plates on a black shield, but that the plates were changed to mice when Gerald de Wimsey advised King Edward I to besiege a castle like a cat at a mousehole— persistently!

Dorothy and Scott-Giles continued letter by letter to invent stories to account for the Wimseys' past. At all times they maintained a serious manner appropriate to "scholarly" study. They finally worked out a family tree that began with the Norman Conquest in 1066. After her death, Scott-Giles corrected any historical errors he found in their work and in 1977 published the family history in a volume called *The Wimsey Family*.

While she was enjoying herself with her close friends, Dorothy was also involved in the social life of literary London. She described it amusingly through the eyes of her character Harriet Vane who in town

> saw her agent and publisher, signed a contract for serial rights, heard the inner history of the quarrel between Lord Gobbersleigh, the newspaper proprietor, and Mr. Adrian Cloot, the reviewer, entered warmly into the triangular dispute raging among Gargantua Colour-Talkies, Ltd., Mr. Garrick Drury, the actor, and Mrs. Smell-Wilmington, author of Passion-Flower Pie, and into the details of Miss Sugar Toobin's monstrous libel action against the *Daily Headline,* and was, of course, passionately interested to learn that Jacqueline Squills had made a malicious expose of her second divorced hus-

band's habits and character in her new novel, *Gas-Filed Bulbs*.

Harriet then goes to a cocktail party where, "the room . . . was exceedingly hot and crowded, and all the assembled authors were discussing (a) publishers (b) agents (c) their own sales (d) other people's sales and (e) the extraordinary behavior of the Book of the Moment selectors in awarding their . . . crown . . . to *Mock Turtle*."

Dorothy might poke fun at her professional social contacts, but she fell madly in love with the professional theater and all its works. She became personally involved with it because she was at a point in her own career when she could not quite decide what to do next. On the one hand, she was enjoying the academic recognition she was getting and she wanted to complete her critical study of Wilkie Collins. But she also had been working on a "straight" novel called *Cat O'Mary*, which she meant to publish under the pen name of Johanna Leigh. In 1935, while she deliberated, there had been an English movie about Lord Peter called "The Silent Passenger." It was based on a story by Dorothy. Since her books had always been full of dialogue, it seemed likely that she herself could write a play. Other people were trying to get the right to "dramatize" Lord Peter too.

Dorothy arrived for dinner one night at Muriel Byrne's full of conversation about a very funny chimney sweep she had just met, worth putting in a story. Much later that evening, after a great deal more talk, Muriel persuaded Dorothy to try writing a play about Lord Peter and her chimney sweep. She got Dorothy to agree by promising to work on the play with her.

Their method of working together was for Dorothy to write a portion of the play and send it over to Muriel, who would rearrange it, cut out the parts that could not be used in a play, and send it back. Their plan was not only to show Lord Peter and Harriet's fans how their romance worked out, but to use this play as an experiment. They wanted it to show the difference between a "thriller" and a psychological crime story, and they wanted to observe the "fair-play" rule to which the Detection Club swore allegiance.

The rule said that the audience must be given all the clues at the same time as the detective, so that they have an equal chance to solve the mystery. They worked out a plot in which all the action takes place in the living room at Talboys, the Wimsey country house, where the clues to the murder could be shown to the audience visually. Then in the second act, although most of the dialogue seems to be about motives, the audience and Lord Peter are learning who had a chance to do the murder. As Lord Peter says to Harriet, "HOW is the only real question. When you know HOW you know WHO"; and Harriet says, "Good heavens! I've married my one Intelligent Reader!" In Act III the playwrights tried to combine a detective novel with a comedy of manners onstage.

Their play, called *Busman's Honeymoon*, opened in London's West End on December 16th, 1936, in the Comedy Theatre. It had powerful competition in the West End, for T. S. Eliot's *Murder in the Cathedral* was also there, along with a Ratigan play, Shakespeare, and other works. But it was a great success, despite some reviewers who gave away the plot and got irate letters to *The Times* from nearly all Dorothy's and Muriel's friends. Along with the royalties from her mysteries, *Busman's Honeymoon* made it possible for Dorothy to plan on having her day-to-day living expenses covered. More than that, it reintroduced her to her lifelong enthusiasm—the stage.

She threw herself into its world with her usual zest and quickly picked up all the jargon, expertise—and gossip. She found the atmosphere and the people very congenial and even more fun than advertising. She enjoyed the work of producing a play so much she could not bear to stay away and was sometimes a nuisance. On the other hand, she also made a great fuss over everyone connected with any play of hers, giving them first night presents and thanking everyone personally when the run was over. She said that part of the charm of playwriting was to see what she had written come alive; she did not dislike or resent the fact that an actor might do something with a character she had not anticipated—she felt it made the stage the closest to real life. As a playwright she was truly like God the creator, making his creatures but allowing them to be themselves.

Val Gielgud, who later produced her plays *The Man Born to Be King* for the B.B.C., said at her death that Dorothy had always seen the theater through rose-colored glasses. Undoubtedly she did, but she also knew a lot about the craft of writing and could be very professional. She saw too that behind all the mechanics which a dramatist ignored at his peril, there was a close, living relationship still between religion and the drama that had come from it, and it was in the theater that she found the kind of community a church is meant to be.

9

RELIGIOUS DRAMATIST

BY 1937 DOROTHY WAS A CELEBRITY. SHE WAS ASKED TO write guest editorials for the London *Times* on such subjects as "Plain English," and she gave many talks about detective fiction or any other topic suggested to her. Like many popular authors, she was also asked to go on lecture tours to America. But Dorothy was not particularly fond of travel, and she felt that her responsibilities at home made it impossible for her to leave. She was very good about writing to her fans, many of whom sent her both letters and presents.

But more and more Dorothy worried aloud about whether writing crime stories was the right use of her talents. On the one hand she argued that detective novels were the most moral literature written, because crime is always punished; and in a speech in February 1939 she also pointed out that it was better to work off one's murderous impulses in reading than otherwise.

Still, she disliked the oversimplification of plot and character typical of mysteries. In fact, in her novel version of *Busman's Honeymoon,* which came out in 1938, she actually carries the story to the bitter end, the night when the murderer is hanged, showing Lord Peter and Harriet struggling morally to accept their roles as "executioners." Furthermore,

Dorothy wondered if it would be true that her books gave weak people ideas for crimes, or if she were adding to a public love of violence for its own sake. This concern went back to her dread of manipulating people's minds and emotions: she wanted individuals to think for themselves. Her basic professional uncertainty is illustrated by the fact that while she wrote more Lord Peter stories after *Busman's Honeymoon*, over half are puzzles with a friendly look into the Wimsey homelife, and her last novel about the Wimseys, to be called *Thrones, Dominations*, was found among her papers incomplete. It is about the marriage of Harriet and Lord Peter in relation to the society about them—very much a comedy of manners, and in nearly two hundred pages has no corpse.

At the same time Dorothy had always based her mysteries squarely upon her own assumptions about the world and human nature. She had been reared and she remained a practicing Christian. Unlike many fellow intellectuals, including her hero G. K. Chesterton, she did not have an adult conversion experience. She never left the Church of England—to rejoin it later. Nor did she join the Church of Rome, although her views on church doctrine made her a spokesman for Roman Catholics and Eastern Orthodox as well as Anglo-Catholics. She never publicized some "made-up" religion of her own, either, no matter what some critics with no knowledge of Christianity may say to the contrary. But Dorothy did work her way through an adolescent mistrust of an emotionally pious and sentimental Christianity that paid no attention to the historic Christian creeds which were the source of its own faith. Like Lord Peter, she was enough of an 18th-century "rationalist" to dislike "enthusiasm." With the help of Chesterton and other writers like him, she became convinced that the "dogma is the drama" of Christianity. Being a Christian became an intellectual adventure for her, one that she pursued with all her heart and with all her soul and with all her mind.

After she arrived in London, Dorothy began to attend

services at a nearby church. Before the bombing of World War II, London was a city filled with small, beautiful parish churches. Dorothy went to St. Thomas, Regent's Street. How often she went no one knows, but for the most part she probably kept the habit she had most of her life of going to church alone and getting up to go to the early service of Holy Communion rather than going later for Morning Prayer with hymns and sermon. She was also an early communicant at All Souls', Witham, when she was in the country.

It was through St. Thomas that Dorothy met other Anglicans such as T. S. Eliot or Charles Williams, both of whom were not only editors in London publishing houses but also writers. The Reverend Patrick McLaughlin, vicar of St. Anne's, Soho, a parish affiliated with St. Thomas, recruited all three of them to help him run a discussion group to lure the unchurched young intellectuals of London. This mission was called the Society of St. Anne's.

Her friendship with Williams, as well as with C. S. Lewis, to whom she first wrote a fan letter about one of his books, has given rise to the mistaken idea that Dorothy was a member of the so-called Inklings. This was an informal, completely male group which met in Oxford during and after the Second World War for much the same reason as the M.A.S.— they came to hear and criticize each other's writing. Its most famous products were Tolkien's *Hobbit* and *Lord of the Rings*, and Lewis's *Narnia* books. The group included, among others, Lewis and his brother, Tolkien, and later, Williams. Since several of the group were also Christian apologists, the name of the group, which they did not use much themselves, has become associated with all the writers who shared their interest in Christianity.

Dorothy had met Charles Williams around 1938. Like many people who became acquainted with her, he occasionally found her almost too energetic and a bit overwhelming, despite the fact that he too was known for his mannerisms and dramatic ways. Dorothy occasionally came by and met him at Amen House, the Oxford University Press offices where he worked, and from there they would go off to a wine bar or some place where they could sit and talk for hours about religion and literature. He was less inclined than Dorothy to lay down the law to other people, and he used to warn her she must remember that dogma itself is really "man-made." She also, inevitably, wrote him long letters, and later on she saw him when she came to Oxford during the war. She also became acquainted with his wife and son and remained in touch with them the rest of her life.

Just as she was wondering what to take on next—whether to go back and finish her Collins' study or *Cat O'Mary* or the novel about the married Wimseys—Dorothy was asked to do something very different from what her public expected her to do. She was offered a chance to do a kind of writing she had not done professionally since her days at Oxford.

The Dean of Canterbury Cathedral was the Reverend George Bell, who later became Bishop of Chichester and an important figure in the World Council of Churches. Canterbury Cathedral is the most important, as well as one of the most beautiful, gothic cathedrals in England. In 1931, Dean Bell, who lived in Canterbury and ran the diocese, while the archbishop lived in London at his palace of Lambeth, organized a group called the Friends of the Cathedral. They began to put on a yearly festival to attract visitors. Among other activities, they produced plays in the cathedral chapter house, which is the meeting place for the Cathedral clergy. Theater festivals were very popular during the 30s when there were Shaw and Shakespeare and Coward festivals. George Bell wanted to put the church and the modern theater world in touch again. His Cathedral plays had only semi-professional casts and short runs, but he wanted good plays and allowed no "Church" censorship.

In 1935 they asked T. S. Eliot, who was at the height of

his influence on the postwar generation both as poet and critic, to write them a new play. (He had become a British citizen and joined the Church of England in 1927.) To write his play Eliot went to the sources of modern drama, which were classical Greek tragedies and medieval mystery plays—both theater that originated in religious worship. The result was his famous *Murder in the Cathedral*, a highly formal play with a chorus onstage and written in blank verse. But it made the murder of Thomas à Becket, a 12th-century Archbishop of Canterbury, seem both modern and vital. *Murder in the Cathedral* was very successful and went from Canterbury to London's West End.

Next, in 1936, the Friends of Canterbury asked Dorothy's friend Charles Williams to write their play. Williams was not only an editor but a lecturer at the City Literary Institute and a prolific writer of criticism, biography, poetry, and "supernatural" thrillers. He was self-educated and spoke with the lower-class accent of East London instead of Oxford's clipped speech. His chief work was a series of poems about King Arthur, written in an original and difficult style, while one of the passions of his life was the medieval Italian poet Dante. For their festival he wrote a verse play about Archbishop Thomas Cranmer, who helped King Henry VIII break away from the Church of Rome, wrote the *Book of Common Prayer*, and was burned at the stake during the reign of Queen Mary.

Dean Bell next asked Margaret Babington to call upon Dorothy and ask her to write the festival play for 1937. It was an honor, but uncharacteristically, Dorothy at first refused, saying she would not "mug" up the history of kings and archbishops. But when Miss Babington explained that the 1937 festival was to be in honor of the arts and crafts that had built the great cathedral, Dorothy agreed, much to the surprise of her public and the press.

Having agreed, Dorothy began to dig about in the Canterbury archives to find a good subject. She knew that since she specialized in crime everyone would expect her to write about murders among the archbishops. But in a Latin chronicle written by Gervase the Monk she found instead an account of the great fire that destroyed the Norman choir section of the cathedral in 1174. After the fire, the chapter of monks voted to hire a foreign architect, William of Sens, to rebuild it. According to Gervase, however, William fell from the scaffolding of the great arch, perhaps due to the "vengeance" of God or the "envy" of the Devil. Here Dorothy had found a historical story suggesting that William of Sens was a great artist in whom pride had gone before a fall—literal and metaphysical—and in her play she has William declare:

> "We are the master-craftsmen, God and I—
> We understand one another...
> And were I lost, something unique were lost
> Irreparably."

This blasphemy is followed by his accident, which is shown as half-natural, half-supernatural. Onstage with the realistic monks who represent Canterbury's chapter (or monastery), Dorothy put four impressive archangels who act as chorus and show that God is acting in the affairs of men. It is Michael the archangel who draws his flaming sword and cuts the windlass rope at the flaw which was overlooked by the workmen.

Her play was called *The Zeal of Thy House*, from Psalm 69. Through her careful plotting, in which William of Sens' dramatic fall from grace is the means by which he comes to a truer understanding of himself and his Creator, Dorothy's own personality and realism peep through. The archangels who frame the human action onstage speak in verse when announcing the will of God, but use ordinary language when they discuss men among themselves. A small cherub asks why God made both men and women since it seems to cause so much trouble on earth. All four archangels tell the cherub roundly that angels never ask "why." Men asked "why" and look what happened to them.

Margaret Babington once asked Dorothy if it had taken a lot of research to make the chapter monks so realistic, but Dorothy said that she had only to recall the last committee meeting she had gone to and use that as a model. Dorothy herself was amused by the reviews which insisted that "not by one line or phrase" can we see the creator of Lord Peter— when in fact the themes of *Gaudy Night* and *The Zeal of Thy House* are identical: the idea that the integrity of the work can redeem personal weakness and vanity.

Dorothy had a marvellous time helping with the play's production. She assisted the director and producer with casting and coaching the half-professional, half-amateur cast. She hunted up props and helped sew the costumes. She insisted that the archangels must not be pretty but terrifying. In the original Canterbury production they stood eleven feet high from sandals to wing tips and were clad in glittering robes of gold cloth. They had gigantic feathered wings over six feet tall, and Dorothy helped sew on the feathers. Someone later asked her if the angels had been chosen from devout Christians, and she retorted that in casting a play the proper Christian approach was to consider actors who were suitable for the parts. First, they must be tall and able to stand for several hours and speak their lines effectively. Then perhaps the director might consider their moral character, not so much whether they went to church regularly as whether they turned up at curtain time and weren't drunk. Even a very immoral actor, if he did not upset the rest of the cast with his behavior, was better than a pious one who could not act. She resolutely refused to make ridiculous distinctions between the "Christian" and the "secular" life.

In late 1938, when *The Zeal of Thy House* was on tour, she wrote a tart letter to the *Times*, which had scolded her publicly for allowing her name to appear in an advertisement for malted milk. She replied that both she and Lord Peter had worked in advertising before, and that she needed the money for *The Zeal of Thy House*. Since she had already contributed as much as she could afford to its tour, and the church in whose honor the play was being performed could not afford to help out, she was "unblushingly" soaking Mammon for what she could get.

The architect William of Sens was played by the actor Harcourt Williams, who helped Frank Napier produce the play at Canterbury in June 1937 and at the Westminster Theater in London in March 1938. Dorothy became very fond of both actors and left them the rights to the play in her will. When the play moved to the West End, all the actors had to be professionals, and some of them still acting remember Dorothy energetically backstage. Her play was a great success both at Canterbury and in London.

During Lent in 1938 Dorothy wrote a Sunday editorial for the *Times*. In it for the first time she proclaimed her own belief that the Christian story as outlined in the historic creeds is the "greatest drama ever staged." She wrote, perhaps with Chesterton in mind:

> Official Christianity... has been having what is known as a bad press. We are constantly assured that the churches are empty because preachers insist too much upon doctrine.... The fact is the precise opposite.... The Christian faith is the most exciting drama that ever staggered the imagination of man... and the dogma is the drama.

She then went on to note that the creeds claimed that Jesus in fact and in truth was the God by whom the universe was created. Because they thought He talked too much and said too many things that were true, the leaders and intellectuals shut Him up by trying Him on a trumped up charge and hanging Him. "All of this was not very creditable even if He was... only a harmless crazy preacher. But if the Church is right about Him, it was more discreditable still, for the man we hanged was God Almighty."

Her next editorial appeared on Easter Sunday, and in it

she accused the religious leaders of the world of being careful not to say anything that might not be understood, with the result that they never said anything at all. This, she charged, was the old sin called laziness. She then went on to discuss the topic which became her major interest the rest of her life:

> Why should God, if there is a God, create anything? . . . That is the real mystery, and probably the only insoluble mystery there is. . . . The Church asserts that there is a Mind which made the universe, that He made it because He is the sort of Mind that takes pleasure in creation, and that if we want to know what the Mind of the Creator is, we must look at Christ.

The more she took public positions, the more her opinion was asked. A woman's society, assuming she was a feminist, asked her to speak. Dorothy told them exactly what her position was in a speech called "Are Women Human?" She told her audience that the day was past when aggressive feminists were going to do much good. She did not like slogans which tried to settle delicate human relationships, and she felt it was wrong to treat any human being as a member of a class instead of as an individual.

Having put the Women's Rightists in their place, she then relented and became very witty about "women." She resented the idea that there was a woman's point of view on income tax or foreign policy, and hoped that women one day would be allowed to have various opinions. "It is my experience," she said, "that both men and women are fundamentally human, and that there is very little mystery about either sex, except the exasperating mysteriousness of human beings in general. . . . I am sure the time has now come to insist . . . on each woman's requirement as an individual person."

For several years after her quarrel with the B.B.C. Dorothy had not written for radio. The success of *The Zeal of Thy House*, however, led Dr. J. W. Welch, who was the head of the B.B.C.'s religious broadcasting, to ask Dorothy to write a nativity play. It was to be broadcast on Christmas Day 1938. Dorothy promptly agreed, but said she must be allowed to write the play realistically, so that it would sound as if the story it was telling was true, not a beautiful church ceremony. The B.B.C. agreed, and the play *He That Should Come* was a great success, both with the critics, who called it arresting, and with the public. The producer of *He That Should Come* was Val Gielgud, brother of the great Shakespearean actor Sir John Gielgud, who became Dorothy's lifelong friend and admirer.

In her introduction Dorothy explained that she wanted to show Christ's birth against the crowded social conditions of His own time. The entire play takes place in the inn courtyard at Bethlehem, which is filled with travelers of every kind. It is not the traditional cave or stable, but a real Eastern inn with a huge platform in the center where travelers lay down with their baggage, while their animals were kept near the great inn gate.

The Three Wise Men speak the prologue and then return after the shepherds to say that the miracle that changed the whole course of human life happened in a world like ours, absorbed in its own affairs and completely unaware of what was happening.

The principal characters are a fussy rich merchant, a Greek, a skinny Pharisee, a rich young Jew named Joseph of Arimathaea, and a Roman centurion. Only a few of the people in the inn hear the angel chorus or understand what is going on, although they know a baby is born.

The Greek says scornfully that when one more child is born everybody is delighted, no matter how unsatisfactory the world is; the young Jew Joseph agrees that all parents think their child will turn out well, when he will probably end up crucified between two thieves. But Joseph also tells Mary that if he should meet her son again, he will have a rich gift for him. As she does so effectively in her plays on the life of

Christ, Dorothy makes use of the tragic irony of the story to give her play depth.

Dorothy was now launched upon a second radio career. During 1939 she participated in a series called "Christ of the Creeds," and she gave talks for the Empire Service broadcast overseas and for the Woman's Hour. Some of these talks were later published in *Unpopular Opinions*, so called by her because a few of the essays are speeches the B.B.C. turned down because they were too outspoken. In January 1939 she was elected president of the Modern Language Association, which she continued to be until 1945. During the late 30's and early 40's a number of her Lord Peter short stories were also broadcast on the B.B.C.

While she was establishing herself in the public eye as a spokesman not only on crime but also on Christianity, Dorothy had been asked to write another play for the 1939 Canterbury Festival. This time she chose to do the exact opposite of what she had done in her first Canterbury play. She used the purely legendary story of Faust, the educated man who sold his soul to the Devil in return for long life, riches, and power. The story dates back to the 16th century, when men first felt that through science and exploration they could all become like God. The Faust legend itself is a weird jumble of magic, superstition, religion, and mythology, with a Devil who is half fallen Satan, half the Greek god Pan.

Dorothy set her play on a traditional Renaissance stage, with the gates of heaven on one side, the mouth of hell on the other, and the mansions of earth in between; she called her play *The Devil to Pay*.

As she pointed out, the Devil is always likely to steal the show, but it is the author's job to keep him under control, even if he is naturally an attractive fellow. The result was her character Mephistopheles, who pops out of hell with a clap of flame and thunder, wearing a lion's head, a snake's tail, and hoofs, but who is witty, sarcastic, and modern. When Faustus asks to be made young and handsome, Mephistopheles grants the wish, but then quickly changes him back again. Faustus yells out,

"Hell and confusion! Damned, damned juggling tricks. Nothing but sorcery!"—to which Mephistopheles replies airily,

"What did you expect when you called me up?"

The original Faust legend has it that he sold his soul for power and knowledge, but Dorothy did not feel the greatest evil in our time is directed towards gaining knowledge for its own sake. She saw Faustus as the impulsive reformer who believed revolution could change everything for the better, but gave up when he found it did not work out. Her Faustus is a kind of Judas Iscariot—brilliant, with great intentions, but a man who destroys himself and others in the name of humanity. The powers Faustus is granted are those the Devil promised Christ in the wilderness: bread, power, and eternal life. The theme of her play therefore is that evil itself is not real, but is the back side of good—good gone wrong. In its closing scene before the Judge of heaven and earth, she has Faustus ask Mephistopheles,

"Who made thee?"

"God; as the light makes the shadow. . . . I am the price that all things pay for being,/The shadow on the world, thrown by the world,/standing in its own light, which light God is."

The Devil to Pay was not as successful as *The Zeal of Thy House,* partly because Faustus was not as sympathetic a character as the arrogant architect, William of Sens, who was a craftsman, not a politician. This play also suffers by comparison with Christopher Marlowe's *Dr. Faustus.* Furthermore, like the devil he is, her Mephistopheles did tend to steal the show. But this play also went from Canterbury to London, where it played four weeks.

10

MASTERPIECE

WHILE DOROTHY HAD BEEN PURSUING A SUCCESSFUL literary career, Great Britain was living through a series of troubles. During the 1930's, the Great Depression had put millions of people out of work. The old king George V had died, and the Prince of Wales, now Edward VIII, had reigned only a few months before abdicating because the Church of England would not allow him to marry a divorced woman. Dorothy commented that Edward VIII was like the legendary epic hero Aeneas of Troy, who fell in love with Dido, Queen of Carthage. She wanted him to stay with her, but his destiny was to found Rome and he could not have both. Most important of all, during the 30's war clouds were gathering across Europe again. Adolf Hitler had come to power as a dictator in Germany. By March 1939 he had marched into Czechoslovakia, and the rest of the world had let him conquer it. Many people continued to hope, however, that postwar treaties and the League of Nations would prevent a major conflict.

The anniversary of World War I occurred on August 4th in an England where the local Civil Defense was already handing out leaflets on how to evacuate children from the cities, how to wear a gas mask, or how to cover windows for blackout. In mid-August Hitler and Stalin, the dictator of Communist Russia, signed a pact to divide up Poland, and by August 25th Hitler was moving his army towards the border. In England over a million mothers, children, and invalids were preparing to leave London on September 1st, the day Hitler invaded Poland. The British government sent him an ultimatum to leave by September 3rd at 11 a.m. He did not reply, and at 11:15 a.m. the Prime Minister went on the B.B.C. to say that Great Britain was at war.

The day-to-day circumstances of everyone's life now were changed, even more so than during the period of the First World War. Mothers and children were sent to the country, stained glass was taken down and stored in safe places, historic buildings like Westminster Abbey were sandbagged against bombing, while businesses like the Oxford University Press and the children's program of the B.B.C. were moved out of London. All streetlights were turned off and air raid drills became a regular part of life, together with the rationing of food and clothing, and the drafting of all able-bodied men and women into war jobs.

Dorothy and her friends found themselves busier than ever. Charis Frankenburg had an entire hospital evacuated to her home, where she helped administer it. Her three sons were all in the armed forces, and the youngest was killed in action in 1942. Muriel Byrne spent a large part of her time replacing a literature professor at Cambridge, commuting back and forth from London in a big old car filled with many of the valuable documents with which she was doing research. At times she stayed with Dorothy and Mac in Witham. Dorothy Rowe stayed in Charis Frankenburg's London flat and acted as an air raid warden in Paddington, while Helen Simpson decided that it was time scholars and poets took part in political life again and offered to run for a seat in Parliament for the tiny Liberal Party. She canvassed a rural district on the Isle of Wight in a pony cart, which she thought was a good contrast with the chauffeur-driven Tories and the air-traveling Laborites.

Dorothy herself, as a writer who was known to be very persuasive, was suggested for a job in the Ministry of Information. She was interviewed, but not hired because she was considered to be too talkative and opinionated. She was, however, increasingly involved in the daily difficulties and dangers of civilian life, for this was a war that was waged on the civilian populations of Britain and Germany, with London and Berlin being two main targets. Her weekend home in Witham was near a large airbase at Colchester.

Like other intellectuals, Dorothy felt called upon to explain what had caused this new war and why the world had failed to preserve the peace won in 1918. She was also concerned about the country's plans once the war was over. Some English writers became very warlike, hating the enemy, while others remained committed to pacifism, even though the government mistrusted them and kept them from important jobs.

Dorothy developed her own position. Her attitude toward the war was that like everything else in the history of man, war is not an end but a beginning. Having gotten into this grim situation, England must aim first to free the world from an intolerable evil. Any good that came out of the war must be the result of individual Englishmen taking stock of themselves. She wanted the public to become more responsible, not allowing their leaders to do their thinking for them, as their enemies had allowed their leaders to do. Her approach was based upon her understanding of history and also upon Christian doctrine. While it is not possible to have heaven on earth, individuals do, she insisted, have the chance to choose how they will act in every situation.

The Sunday after war had been declared, the *Sunday Times* printed one of her guest editorials, entitled "What Do We Believe?" In it she remarks that a faith is not meant to be a comfort to us in bad times, but a truth about ourselves. Christians are saved *through* danger and suffering, not *from* them. But there will be no end to the creative life, which one way or another will continue to make things. Groups and nations are not the way to salvation, especially if they leave the individual no creative responsibility for his own life. As often happened, critics took these statements as her own invention instead of as Christian doctrine.

During the restless winter of 1939 called the "Phony War," when Hitler kept saying he was going to bomb Britain or invade her but did neither, Dorothy wrote a series of weekly articles for *The Spectator*. They were called the "Wimsey Papers," and each article consisted of several short letters from different members of the Wimsey family or friends. In one, for example, the dowager duchess describes how pleasant it is to have her daughter-in-law in London working for the Ministry of Instruction and Morale. Lord St. George is in the R.A.F. flying fighters, while the women in Miss Climpson's Cattery, Lord Peter's detective bureau, are listening to rumors on the Home Front to check on civilian morale.

Lord Peter is by far the most serious. He is back in Army Intelligence, slipping in and out of countries across the Channel, aware that with a wife and two sons he is no longer "free" to get killed. He is amused and appalled by his brother the duke, who is planting baby oaks on the estate without any idea whether there will be any future for dukedoms. Peter cannot see the aristocratic way of life as something to fight for, but he has been arguing with a Laborite who believes that man can achieve economic equality and individual liberty at the same time.

These letters also gave tips on how to cross a blacked-out street without being hit by a car, described homefront air raid drills, and discussed the troubles of teaching children evacuated from the big cities without any school books, paper, pencils, or desks. In 1943 Dorothy gave a talk on England's laws to the Girls Training Corps, which was part of the local secondary school at Witham. This school had another school evacuated to it, and Dorothy not only invited the girls to come visit her—an invitation not made lightly—but she also had one of their evacuated masters lodged at her house and let him use her library.

"The Wimsey Papers" are a very interesting commentary on the first winter of war. They also dramatize Dorothy's own conclusions. Harriet writes to Peter that she is "terrified by this . . . demand for an 'enduring peace'. . . . We might have prevented this war, if it hadn't been for our inflexible will to peace." She was remembering when the League of Nations allowed Mussolini to conquer Ethiopia and when the British Prime Minister Chamberlain agreed in Munich to let Hitler "keep" Czechoslovakia and came home to say that he had saved "peace in our time."

The Spectator articles ended abruptly on January 26, 1940, with the statement that they would no longer appear weekly; they in fact never appeared again. Dorothy had annoyed either the public or the editorial board, or just possibly the government, which may have been afraid to hire her because she would speak her mind. She felt the public had a right to know what was going on and loudly resented the wartime propaganda methods being used to control opinion. Her attitude never changed—she simply found other places to express it.

Early in 1940 Gollancz published a long wartime essay called *Begin Here,* and the book had good reviews. One critic called it a "lively sermon" and added that nothing Dorothy wrote was ever dull. Another said that *Begin Here* was as readable as Lord Peter and a lot more stimulating. But the intriguing thing about the book is that it is a clear restatement of the very ideas she had been expressing in "The Wimsey Papers."

What she was saying again was that it was necessary to begin now to reconstruct a world in which the poets—by whom she meant all artists and scholars—and the ordinary man had not lost touch with each other. She said that the poet, who "stands for the expression of the Whole Man—for the life of the body and of the mind"—is needed by the ordinary man because he helps him fulfill his individual potential. Man cannot go back to being innocent or savage, he must be made whole again by knowledge and understanding of himself.

In the midst of war in April 1940 Dorothy's romantic comedy *Love All* was produced in London at the Torch Theatre and had pleasant reviews. The notices gave her credit for putting the case for women's rights very amusingly in this play about a philandering novelist and his playwright wife. But Dorothy's real creative interest at the moment was reflected in her speeches, which were often published later as wartime pamphlets.

One of them was called "The Mysterious English." In it she explains that the true Englishman is a mongrel, without a real folk custom or costume and with a language which is a compound of Anglo-Saxon and Norman French. The English are bound together by their common law and the fact that they became a nation very early. Dorothy added that Hitler would not bomb them into submission because every Englishman sees himself as defending *his* rights, *his* island; he is the mongrel guarding his own door. Hitler did not, of course, win the so-called Battle of Britain.

In 1941, when she was close to fifty, Dorothy began work on a new kind of project. A series of books called Bridgeheads was planned to help the country cope with the unpleasant realities of wartime. Dorothy's friend Muriel Byrne was to write one on privilege and responsibility, while Dorothy wrote another on the nature of creation as a demonstration of God. Her book was called *The Mind of the Maker*.

The Mind of the Maker represents Dorothy's understanding of the creative process. It is a commentary, based upon her own experience, on the statements made in the Christian creeds. Again, she insists that her modern readers must understand that she is not making up a religion to fit her experience as an author, but the other way around: her experience as a writer has made the Christian statements about God make sense to her. Her critics, who have tended to be scientifically oriented people, resent Dorothy's insistence that theology is also an exact science with a specific vocabulary of its own which must be clearly defined for any discussion to be worthwhile. But in this book she is illustrating the meaning of the creeds, not trying to prove their truth. She felt therefore that she had as much right to take certain statements for granted as any other scientist who was testing a hypothesis.

In this book she used many examples from her own writing, but basic to her whole discussion is her understanding of God as a maker or artist. The characteristic common to God and man is the desire and ability to make things. To Dorothy, we are most alive when we are using that power, each in his or her own way.

Towards the end of *The Mind of the Maker*, Dorothy stated clearly her understanding of her own career, saying,

> At the day's end or the year's end [the artist] . . . may tell himself: the work is done. But he knows in his heart that it is not, and that the passion for making will seize him again . . . and drive him to construct a fresh world. And though he may imagine for the moment that this fresh world is wholly unconnected with the world he has just finished, yet, if he looks back along the sequence of his creatures, he will find that each was in some way the outcome and fullfillment of the rest—that all his worlds belong to the one universe.

Dorothy was involved with other aspects of the war besides its philosophical concerns. She complained publicly about the B.B.C.'s habit of putting religious programs on just before or after the news, so that one got prayed at whether or not one wanted to be. She and Helen Simpson wrote a letter to *The Times* insisting that it was perfectly logical to keep the London churches open but close the theaters during the war since many Christians had a duty to attend church. Then she really blew up over the fact that a news commentator for the B.B.C. referred to P. G. Wodehouse as a traitor because after the Americans saved him from being interned in France by the Germans, he made some broadcasts to America talking about conditions in occupied France. Everyone apologized eventually to Wodehouse, who went to America and stayed there, but Dorothy was one of the few to defend him at once. Shortly afterwards, Dorothy suffered a personal blow when her friend Helen Simpson died in October. She wrote a delightful, loving appreciation of Helen for *The Spectator,* to which they had both so often been contributors.

In mid-1940 Dorothy was again approached by the religious department of the B.B.C. Dr. Welch wanted her to do a series for the Children's Hour on the life of Christ. But the B.B.C. had moved many of its departments to Bristol to escape the bombing (which they had plenty of there), and Dorothy did not want to travel that far. But she finally agreed to write the series of plays on two conditions. She must be allowed to write these plays in modern English, and Jesus Himself must appear onstage.

In England there is an old law that the person of Christ may not be acted onstage. The Director-General of the B.B.C., however, got permission from the Lord Chamberlain for Dorothy to use Christ as a character because He would only be heard, not seen. Dorothy also wanted Val Gielgud to produce the plays, but instead got the director of the Children's Hour. He and Dorothy had a running battle by mail over who was in charge of the operation. She also wrote Dr. Welch long letters, telling him about her problems and progress, and they became good friends. Much of what she wrote him is included in the introductions to the published plays.

Dorothy's first move was to give the series a "fairytale" title which told the whole story: "The Man Born to be King." Like many of her titles, it is also a literary quotation—this one from a short story by William Morris. No one in modern times had written such a play, although at Oberammergau in Germany there is a tradition of acting out the Passion story every ten years, with local citizens taking the parts. Dorothy's job was to write a series of plays to be broadcast a month apart. Some of her audience might hear only one or two; others might listen faithfully to the whole series. (As it happened, when the plays were produced they were put into an adult time slot and became the talk of the island.)

Medieval mystery plays, although she used them for suggestions, were too remote to be good models to work from, and they had huge casts with each character standing for a single trait or event. But there was one cycle of stories with which she had been familiar since her childhood—the legends about King Arthur and his knights of the Round Table, known in literature as the "matter of Britain." Like the life of Christ, King Arthur's story has a dramatic birth, which leads to his secret upbringing by Merlin and his recognition as king by the sword in the stone. Then, until the very end when the king is betrayed, there is no central plot at all, only the various adventures of his knights. In this respect, the Arthurian legends are like the Gospel accounts of Christ's life: between the story of Jesus' birth and the story of His passion and death we are not given a sustained chronological story of His life but rather strings of parables, miracles, and sayings which are often organized by subject matter rather than by strict sequence of time. Dorothy called her plays a "cycle" in the sense in which the King Arthur legends are a cycle, but she was determined to give hers a far tighter, more dramatic plot.

She began to work with a Greek New Testament and did her own translating because she wanted to make the speech contemporary. She used the British empire to help her listeners see that the Roman empire was a kind of government they understood, and she had her characters talk in different English accents, from Cockney to Oxford, to show their social status. The unifying theme of these plays is the idea of kingship, or how the world should be ruled. Most important of all, she invented a realistic plot in which the drama comes from the relationship between her two main characters, Jesus Bar (son of) Joseph and Judas Iscariot.

She went through the Gospels and made an outline of the main events, combining any miracles or actions that were basically the same. Then she drew the plot together by using minor characters over and over, such as the Roman centurion Proclus, who appears in most of the plays. She used some traditional identifications—like making Mary who was the sister of Lazarus also Mary Magdalene—and she made all of Christ's major disciples, including Judas, disciples first of John Baptist, so that she could have Peter, James, John, and Judas all appear as early as her second play.

Judas becomes convinced that he alone can bring in the kingdom of God. He is the intellectual who thinks he can use the powers of this world to produce a New Jerusalem without being corrupted. In this belief, he is like Dorothy's Faustus. Dorothy invented a Zealot leader named Baruch, and has him deliberately work on Judas' pride until Judas is convinced that Jesus has betrayed His mission. The Zealots were Jewish guerrillas bent on freeing the Jews from Roman control and who hoped to make use of Jesus.

The reason why the characterization of Judas is so important is that he is used to make the character Jesus Bar Joseph real. Judas is the follower who understands His wit, His arguments, and His ideas. If it had not been for his pride, he, not Peter, might have been the cornerstone of the church or a great apostle to the gentiles like Paul. Judas in Dorothy's plays clearly sees Jesus as a marvelously witty, clever, and compelling person, but he never sees Who He Is.

While she was working hard on these plays, Dorothy and Mac had moved to Witham to live. She had taken over her father's housekeeper when he died, and then during the 30's she had a young couple who left when a second child made the small cottages too cramped. Although she complained often about servant problems, during the war she had another house-keeper, Connie, and someone to look after the garden at least part of the time.

When she was home Dorothy would bathe as soon as she got up (she had a rack built across the tub so she could read or make notes if she wanted to) and have breakfast. Then she dealt with her mail and went to work. Her study was a small room at the front of the house, although her projects tended to overflow into other rooms as they grew.

During the remodeling of the cottages, she had an arch-way built between the two sitting rooms and made herself a library upstairs by throwing the two front bedrooms together. Over the fireplace in the library hung the Wimsey Coat of Arms. While working out a difficult problem she liked to hike up and down the garden in back or work jigsaw puzzles. She rarely appeared downstairs in the house before noon, although when it was cold, she might work in the boiler room near the furnace, where she and the cats also entertained an occasional guest with sherry. Often she and Mac met only to eat dinner together.

Until 1939 she had a secretary named Sheila Lake, who left when the war began. Dorothy then asked a Witham neighbor, Mrs. Richards, if she knew anyone who could help her out. Mrs. Richards said that she would send along one of her daughters. Kathleen Richards worked for Dorothy until the war ended, when her sister took over the job. They helped her with her correspondence, typed her manuscripts, paid her bills (Dorothy rarely carried money and she hated handbags), and gathered her household receipts for the tax man.

They both found working for Dorothy fascinating, but difficult. Sometimes they had to dig out material that needed typing, or decipher her cryptic printer's symbols when answer-ing her mail. Dorothy did a lot of her writing in cheap, paper-covered children's exercise books, sometimes making a fair copy later but often having a typescript made straight from the books. She was not a neat person in her work habits and her bedroom and study usually were a mess, with books and papers all over everything and a cat or two on top. The Richards girls did not work fulltime for Dorothy and came only on evenings and weekends. During the war Kathleen Richards worked elsewhere all day, came to type for Dorothy in the evening, then at 10:30 p.m. went on duty at a first aid station.

When they appeared, Dorothy was usually up and working, either on a project or keeping up her huge correspondence. While food remained scarce during the war and afterwards, her fans sent her all kinds of food parcels. Fancy things like glazed fruit Dorothy often gave to her secretary, but the more nourishing food she shared with some of the local residents, who she felt needed it more than she did.

While Dorothy continued to work furiously, Mac was probably both lonely and bored. His moodiness had increased and his health apparently was not good enough for him to join the civilian defense known as the Home Guard, in which most of the over-age men served. He spent a lot of time at the Red Lion with his friend Mr. Bull, the local photographer. He was still considered very entertaining company, but once put out his cigarette and left when introduced as "Dorothy Sayers' husband."

Mac had a study of his own on the ground floor of Number 22 and a shed in the garden with a north light and a heater where he painted. The Flemings kept chickens as well as pigs to help the wartime food shortages. All the female pigs were called "Fatima" and the males, "Francis Bacon." They were treated like family pets until it came time to butcher them. Dorothy was always upset at slaughter time, and she wrote one Christmas card in Latin literary style in which her cats ponder the fate of the pigs who disappear.

Dorothy hated being interrupted at her work, which often made her seem rude to the Witham community. But the longer she lived there, the more everyone became used to her habits and accepted her. On the streets she greeted everyone she knew with a loud, hearty hello, often ignoring the fact she had forgotten to take off her apron or change her old shoes. She also tried to avoid opening church fetes or taking on community work except as a favor to old friends. Friends of hers or their children or cats came to visit now and then, and Kathleen Richards remembers being asked to describe the local political situation whenever Dorothy's cousin Gerald Sayers came to call.

Dorothy's household always had a cat—or cats—and she was not particular about what kind of cat—she liked them all because of their native pride and independence of character. She was also the favorite aunt of every cat in Witham. There was a cat room at the top of the stairs where every cat in the neighborhood came to have kittens. Dorothy then took the kittens by taxi to London and gave them to her favorite restaurants to be mousers because she did not approve of drowning them. She left her kitchen window open for them at night and once the pipes all froze. Each cat in her household had its own dish, including a big black moocher named Tom, who came only to eat. One year she sent a Christmas card to the Richards' cats from her cats, signed by them all: Bramble, George Macaulay Trevelyan, Sandra, Titty Taldrum, and the Goblin.

Margery Barber had been given a handsome, long-haired white cat called Timothy White who occasionally stayed with his "Aunt Sayers." He once got on the skylight outside the bathroom where Mac was bathing, and when he yelled at the animal, Dorothy and the cleaning woman had to chase him down with poles. Timothy's companion in the Barber-Byrne household was a Scots dog called Bunter whose "Aunt Sayers" once took him to Fortnum's for tea. Timothy died at a great age in October 1948, and Dorothy wrote a poem to him which ends:

> When the Ark of the new life grounds upon Ararat,
> Grant us to carry into the rainbow's light,

In a basket of gratitude, the small, milk-white
Silken identity of Timothy, our cat.

In addition to chickens, pigs, and cats, Aunt Leigh's parrot lived on Newland Street, and Dorothy later adopted another one. It was a gray African parrot with a rose chest named Joey, who had belonged to the pub called The Spread Eagle in Witham. Joey lived in the kitchen, and when the air raid siren went off, he used to shout out, "There it goes again, Con!"

In 1944 Dorothy published an amusing little book of cautionary tales called *Even the Parrot.* It poked fun at a lot of modern theories about daily life, taking up in turn the canary, the cat, the beehive, and the boa constrictor. Each provided an object lesson to the pert youngsters Mathilda and Archibald. The morals of the tales are quite amusing. The cat does not consider kittens a fulltime job and kicks them out as soon as they can cope, while the beehive teaches poor Archibald that there really is no need for men in a well-organized society.

Meanwhile, Dorothy was also working on her plays about Christ. There was trouble about casting the parts, especially that of Christ. The plan was to have all the actors anonymous, but the actors objected. Dorothy's favorite actors were all in the war, but she was determined that the part be played by someone who had a magnificent voice yet did not sound conceited. Finally, Robert Speaight, the actor who had played the archbishop in Eliot's *Murder in the Cathedral,* was chosen. A lot of nasty comments were made about him as someone who thought he could act God Almighty.

Dorothy was also worrying about the length of the scripts, which had been increased from a half hour to forty-five minutes. But the plays were getting written when early in 1941 a producer's assistant sent one back with some suggested changes. Dorothy did not care for anyone to tell her how to improve her plays, and she blew up, tearing her contract into tiny pieces, and mailing it back to the B.B.C. The B.B.C. did not want to give up the project, so they gave in. They even let Dorothy have Val Gielgud as producer, and the plays were given to another B.B.C. department so that Gielgud (and Dorothy) would not have to go to Bristol to produce them.

By December of 1941 Dorothy had finished five plays, the first of which was to be broadcast over Christmas. Dr. Welch decided to hold a press conference and asked Dorothy to be there. She read some of the dialogue and a prepared statement about writing them. Partly because in this kind of public give and take she felt shy and reacted by being abrupt, some of the reporters decided that she was being too offhand with them. For this reason perhaps and because they were hungry for a sensational news story, the reporters gave a very distorted idea of the plays and suggested that they were sacrilegious.

At this point the Lord's Day Observance Society, a very strict Protestant group, began a public attack on Dorothy and the B.B.C. to keep them from broadcasting the plays. Their claim was that the B.B.C. was breaking the Third Commandment, which forbids taking the name of the Lord in vain. They were shortly afterwards joined in their crusade by the Protestant Truth Society.

Petitions were sent to Prime Minster Winston Churchill and to the Archbishop of Canterbury as the head of the Church of England, demanding that they ban the plays. Letters for and against the plays poured into the London newspapers, and the noisy outcries went on to the point at which a member of Parliament named Sir Percy Hurd asked Mr. Ernest Thirkel, the Parliamentary Secretary for the Ministry of Information, a "Question" in the House of Commons. What Sir Percy wanted to know was whether the Ministry was going to revise the plays. The answer was "No."

But the fuss had made the B.B.C. Board of Governors nervous. They decided that they must have the consent of the

Central Religious Advisory Council of the B.B.C., which included members of all the major Christian denominations. Its chairman was the Bishop of Winchester, who later said that these plays were the greatest evangelistic appeal made in the 20th century, although Dorothy herself insisted that "playwrights are not evangelists." Because of the war the council could not get together, so they were sent copies of the plays. All but one voted in favor of them. Still the B.B.C. Board hesitated until finally Dr. Welch wrote them that he had been working for two years on this project, which he thought was Miss Sayers' masterpiece. He added that she was either right or wrong and that he would stand by her.

The first play was broadcast on December 21, 1941, not only in Great Britain, but overseas to the Empire as well. The public reacted just as Dorothy wanted them to do: enthusiastic about the plays and annoyed with the small group who had tried to keep them from hearing them for themselves. The plays became more and more popular as they were broadcast, and the series was a huge success. It was rebroadcast so many times even in Dorothy's lifetime that she made jokes about it, looking forward to the day when the plays were interrupted with commercials for bread or fish, a new wine company, or a carpenter's union. But she was paid only about three thousand dollars for her hard work.

Despite the bombing of London, Dorothy came to many of the rehearsals. She wrote fascinating notes for the producer and the main actors, which were later published with the plays, giving a clear idea of what she wanted to accomplish. She and Mac then listened to the broadcasts at home in Witham and Mac thought they were a "good show." When the plays were published in 1943 Dorothy dedicated them to Val Gielgud, "who has made them his already." In her original introduction she also thanked the Lord's Day Observance Society for "so obligingly doing all our publicity for us."

These plays were a great triumph for Dorothy, but characteristically she made light of the creative power that had gone into their construction. She insisted that the Gospel story was so great that no one could do it justice; but no one could spoil it either—not even a detective novelist and a crew of West End actors. But she had actually created the dramatic structure of the plays, which makes *The Man Born to Be King* much more than just a good job by an honest craftsman.

1942 proved to be the low point of the war for the English. France had fallen in 1940, and the British forces had been rescued from Dunkirk in tatters. Later that year the Battle of Britain had raged over their heads, with bombing every day for two months. In 1941 Hongkong had fallen, and the war was surging into other Far Eastern parts of the British Empire like Malaya, Rangoon, and Singapore. Then Pearl Harbor was bombed and the Americans were also fighting—hopelessly outnumbered—in the Philippines. Britain now had China, Russia, the United States, and her Empire as allies, but everyone was asking how soon Australia and New Zealand would fall, and if the war would reach India and Burma. None of the campaigns against the Axis powers of Germany, Italy, and Japan had been successful.

In this dreadful time Dorothy wrote a poem which was published in November and sent out as her Christmas card. As might be expected, she took a very individualistic approach to the war, making fun of it and herself. The poem is called, "Lord, I Thank Thee." In it she lists all the things about wartime England that suit her. She hates traveling to foreign countries—now she can't. She detests bananas, which are a smug fruit—now she can't get them. She doesn't take sugar in coffee or tea—now she can give hers to her neighbors and be popular. She doesn't have to buy new clothes or change for dinner or make up her face. She finds it jolly to have newspapers thin with no twaddle like the woman's page, while all the ads have shrunk into a shadow of their former selves. There is not enough newsprint even to misquote her, and she hopes that soon no one will report her at all.

11

TRANSLATOR OF DANTE

O<small>N</small> D-DAY, JUNE 6, 1944, THE ALLIES BEGAN THEIR LONG-awaited invasion of Hitler's Europe. The invasion took hold and the march across the continent to Germany began. At the same time, however, the Germans launched a new secret weapon at England—the V-1 plane (followed by the V-2 rocket, one of whose creators was Werner von Braun, who later became a pioneer space scientist in America). The V-1s were pilotless planes which roared like a tugboat. They would appear and keep everyone in suspense until their motors cut out—then they dived to earth with an ominous flash of green light and blew up. Many people were killed or injured by them. Exploded, these robots looked like great dead bats with broken backs.

Since Witham was between Colchester and London, it was often under fire from these "doodle-bugs," as the English called them. While Mac liked to watch the planes or rockets come over, standing out in the garden, Dorothy hated and feared air raids. During a raid her strong visual imagination could dream up all kinds of horrors that had lurked for years in the back of her mind. When the alarm siren sounded, she always went quickly to their cellar shelter, grabbing some book to read as she went.

Before one air raid that summer, when Mac yelled at her to hurry up, she rushed downstairs from her study clutching

the first volume of her grandmother Sayers' Temple edition of
Dante's *Divine Comedy*. These editions were pocket-sized
books bound in limp leather. The Dante had the medieval
Italian text of the poem on one page and a prose English
translation across from it on the opposite page. Dorothy did
not know modern Italian, but with the help of her French and
what Latin she could remember, she managed to read the first
part, *Inferno* (or *Hell*), fairly well. By the time the "all clear"
finally sounded, she was absolutely fascinated by Dante,
whom she had never taken the time to read.

She had in fact been planning to read him ever since
1943, when her friend Charles Williams had published a book
called *The Figure of Beatrice*, which is a critical study of
Dante's understanding of the Christian meaning of romantic
love. Dorothy had already read Williams' book, not because it
was about Dante, but because it was by her friend. His book
had convinced her that Dante was undoubtedly a great poet,
but she still had not rushed off to read him. She had gotten
the Temple edition off the shelf and blown off the dust and
left it lying about, waiting for the perfect moment when she
would feel like tackling 14,000 lines of poetry "full of Guelfs
and Ghibellines and Thomas Aquinas." She had the sneaking
suspicion that she would read about ten cantos and then forget
to finish it.

Instead, reading Dante for the first time at the age of
fifty-one, she found his *Divine Comedy* the most exciting adventure story she had read since Dumas' *The Three Musketeers*.
Nobody had told her that Dante is one of the best storytellers
the world has ever known.

> However foolish it may sound, the plain fact is that I
> bolted my meals, neglected my sleep, work and corre-
> spondence, drove my friends crazy, and paid only a dis-
> tracted attention to the doodle-bugs which happened to
> be infesting the neighborhood at the time, until I had
> panted my way through the Three Realms of the Dead
> from top to bottom and from bottom to top. . . . I discov-

ered that [Dante] . . . was not grim and austere, but sweet and companionable . . . an affable archangel . . . [and] that he was a very great comic writer—which is quite the last thing one would ever have inferred from the things people say in their books.

As she wrote Charles Williams, she was dying to begin a novel with the words "George was curled up comfortably in the big arm-chair, chuckling over the *Divine Comedy*," just to see how many reviewers would write to tell her that the *Divine Comedy* is not funny.

During this later period of the war Dorothy was doing broadcasting, supervising the production of her plays by amateur groups all over England, giving talks, and writing articles as usual. She also had "adopted" two Porter's blackish tortoises at the London Zoo as part of a national effort to help pay for feeding the zoo animals, and bills would come every so often for what the Flemings called the two "blackish portuses." In 1946 she also adopted a Giant Tortoise who is still alive and goes to Whipsnade Zoo for his summer holidays. The Sayers Society has made him an honorary member. Dorothy also went to a lot of trouble to get wartime rations for her pets and the pets of her friends like Val Gielgud.

While busy, Dorothy had not gotten started on a major project again. Then she learned that Dr. E. V. Rieu was editing a group of translations of classics like *The New Testament* and *The Odyssey* for Penguin paperbacks. Early in 1945 she wrote to Dr. Rieu and proposed that she translate Dante's *Divine Comedy* into modern English verse. She planned to use Dante's own three-line stanzas, the terza rima. Already she had taught herself how to read medieval Italian.

She felt the time was ripe for a new, livelier, less "sacred" translation of Dante. She wanted everybody to enjoy the story as well as to understand its meaning. For as she had enthusiastically written Charles Williams,

it is hard to repress Dante. You may squash him, silence him, reduce him to blushes and confusion, but he bobs up again like a cork. . . . Always inquisitive and talkative, he prattles his way through Hell and Purgatory; and as he goes his real charm gets the better of Virgil. . . .

Dorothy approached Dante as one craftsman approaches another. In her many speeches and articles on Dante she gives the impression that she has come into his study and is looking over his shoulder as he writes. To her, as to her friend Williams, an author cannot "die" so long as his work exists, and it is her ability to see Dante "alive in his writing" that is one of her chief claims to fame as a Dante scholar. To her the past is never inferior to the present, and we are not superior to our ancestors just because we are alive today.

There were three things about the *Comedy* that she thought brilliant. First, Dante began his poem where all good adventure stories should begin—right in the middle. Second, as the story went along through Hell, Purgatory, and Heaven, she admired Dante's structure, which made the whole story perfectly clear and yet held her interest. Dante's poem, she noted, was built like a great gothic cathedral. Finally, she recognized that Dante had the trick of creating a universe of living, breathing characters—a real world. Any reader of Dorothy's who has gone to look for the tennis courts in Mecklenburg Square, certain that Harriet Vane must be up-stairs in her apartment deciding whether to go to the Oxford Gaudy, knows what Dorothy meant.

Dorothy's education and recent work had prepared her strikingly well for the Dante project. Even before college she had had a passion for doing verse translation, while more recently she had written verse plays for Canterbury. Fur-thermore, all during the war she had been lecturing and writ-ing on how to rebuild society so that it would allow individuals to develop into true children of God. In *Begin Here* she had suggested that the public make use of its Western-Mediterranean-Christian heritage: Dante was its great spokesman. In *The Mind of the Maker* she had dealt with the craftsman's approach to creation as he mimics God's own creative work. What Dante had to say about people and the state, as well as about the soul and God, seemed to Dorothy the answers the modern world was looking for. The result was that she devoted most of the rest of her professional life to winning an audience for another artist's work.

Dr. Rieu at Penguin Books accepted her offer to do the new translation for him. And from 1946 to 1949 Dorothy was busily at work translating *Hell.* In her opinion many Dante scholars were terribly discouraging because they made the ordinary person feel he could not possibly read Dante for himself. Her own clear, beautifully written introductions and notes try to fill in the gaps in the education of the modern public, which has been brought up on science and psychiatry and television, but is illiterate in history and the classics.

To the dismay of her own public, Dorothy made a firm announcement in 1947 that she would write no more about Lord Peter, and it is clear from her notebooks that this is about the period when she stopped writing even an occasional short story about him and his family. She also had packed away her work on Wilkie Collins and never went back to it.

During the early war years Dorothy's son Anthony was at Malvern College, a secondary school—the same one where C. S. Lewis had been so unhappy because they made him play team sports. Then in 1942 he was admitted to Balliol College at Oxford as the Domus History Scholar. Anthony was registered at both school and college as the only son of Oswald A. Fleming, and many Witham residents assumed he was just that. Inevitably, his education was interrupted by the war, and Anthony did not return to Balliol until 1946. In 1948 he took his degree at Oxford with First Class Honors, like his mother before him.

Dorothy traveled to Oxford occasionally, not only to see Charles Williams and other friends, but also to speak at the Socratic Society, which so impressed her she wanted to start a branch at her parish in London. This society had been started in 1941 by a Somerville student and was presided over by C. S. Lewis until he left to go to Cambridge University. Its purpose was to provide a place where Christians, atheists, and agnostics could discuss their intellectual differences. Members of the other Oxford colleges soon joined Somerville, and it became known as the Oxford Socratic Society. While Lewis was still there to chair the meetings, it became known as a place where students and professors who had never heard Christianity discussed rationally could hear it made interesting and important. Dorothy's efforts to start a similar group in London, however, never quite succeeded.

Both Lewis and Dorothy were doing broadcasts for the B.B.C. Their talks "in defense of Christianity" aroused considerable opposition among certain liberal groups who felt that these two Christians were getting a free platform to explain their "medieval" theology. Lewis's talks were eventually published together under the title *Mere Christianity*. Some of Dorothy's contributions were published in *Unpopular Opinions*, which came out in 1946, and in *Creed or Chaos*, which was published in 1947.

The war ended in 1945, but England, although victorious, was left poor and distressed by the need both to rebuild itself and to help administer a war-torn Europe. Dorothy's old friend Dean Bell, now the Bishop of Chichester, had been part of a group who worked to provide famine relief behind the battle lines, and now he worked to help solve the ghastly problems of the DPs, or displaced persons, wandering all across Europe. Dorothy herself said that the worst war problem would be what to do with the "innocent victims," although no one living was totally innocent or totally guilty. She felt strongly that the English must reestablish a right relationship with their enemies or they would end by destroying themselves. Just as stoutly, however, she refused to agree that the churches must be the source of political or social action to create a brave new world. Echoing the position taken by William Temple, Archbishop of Canterbury during the war, she said that the church's mission in any age is to bear witness *against* the world, both for its vices and for its dangerous virtues. The church continued to need her as a spokesman, and she found it difficult to refuse, even when it took time from her own work.

After the war was over and the Nazi atrocities against their Jewish population became fully known, Dorothy was sometimes accused of anti-Semitism. This accusation was based partly on her novels, where some characters use the slang terms of the period, just as they do in the books of her contemporaries. Another aspect of the problem was that in the postwar mood of guilt over the extermination camps, any Christian who insisted that it was Jews who had helped to judicially murder Christ was labelled anti-Semitic. People were anxious that all of mankind accept responsibility for the sins of particular people, without being willing to distinguish between the generally sinful nature of man and the individual difference between a murderer and a bystander. It is ironic that it is just this kind of linguistic fallacy that Dorothy herself liked to hunt out ruthlessly and exterminate.

So far as her Jewish friends are concerned, the charge is nonsense. Moreover, Dorothy wrote an article about the "Jewish question" which was very serious and foresighted, although not well received in liberal circles at the time. She tried in it to look at the problem of a historically displaced people from the standpoint of the average Englishman who is asked to accept them into his country as fellow citizens. She said that inevitably Jewish refugees from the Continent seemed "foreign" while at the same time she distrusted the idea that the simple solution was to give them a homeland that happened to belong to someone else. She concluded by saying that a Christian must try to understand the whole problem and accept the people too.

When V-E Day ended the war in Europe and before the United States had dropped the atomic bomb to end the war against Japan, the English held a General Election. Winston

Churchill's wartime government was defeated. Most of the world was amazed at this outcome, since Churchill had led the British to victory, but the strains of war and the promises of peace had also made many voters fed up with leaders who had been in charge. It seemed possible to have a whole new world.

But to Dorothy, to whom continuity with the past meant a great deal and whose Christian beliefs did not include belief in progress, Churchill's defeat, together with the rapid breaking up of the British Empire, was totally wrong. She did not think liberty and equality were possible at the same time, nor did she think that economic goals were the same as social or religious goals. She was also deeply concerned over what the machine was doing to men and to nature. Part of her desire to put Dante's message across to her contemporaries came from her wish not to lose the traditional ways of understanding what life is all about.

The new Labor government's emphasis on big government, central planning, state-run industries, and heavy taxation made her feel as if she were living under a dictatorship. So far as she personally was concerned, she could not afford to write another Lord Peter book because it would have cost her more than she made; living on royalties as she worked on Dante was also increasingly difficult.

In June of 1946 another verse play of Dorothy's was presented in the great gothic cathedral at Lichfield as part of the festival held to celebrate the city's 750th anniversary. It is called *The Just Vengeance*. Dorothy wrote to her secretary, Kathleen Richards, that it had gone well the first night, poorly the second—and that when Kathleen came to see it herself, would she please bring Dorothy's academic cap and gown so Dorothy would look less of an ass marching in a church procession that Sunday!

This play was produced by Dorothy's old friend Frank Napier, who also played the part of George Fox, the Quaker. The principal role of the Persona Dei, or God, was played by another old friend, Raf de la Torre. It is a pageant-like play, with a cast of several dozen characters who first represent the people of Lichfield and then citizens of all cities since Adam and Eve. The city is being honored for its long history but also for its symbolic role as "the city," or the City of God. The play's theme came from *Paradiso*, the third book of the *Comedy*, and its title is from the Seventh Canto, where Beatrice tells Dante,

"You are wondering how the just vengeance justly was avenged."

The whole action takes place in the moment when an airman is shot down in the war and his spirit calls out to his city to save him. But then he tries to insist that the future must be good and just, or he will have died in vain. The city shows him, as he is taken into fellowship with all its citizens, past and present, that what he wants is something not even Christ got, and he accepts not only his salvation but the way of the Cross as the only way to achieve it.

Dorothy felt that this play was the best thing she ever wrote. She meant that it was her most successful effort to get across the Christian idea that each person's conscious choice is what determines his salvation. Or, as the Persona Dei says in his last speech,

> *"Shall I not keep faith*
> *Now with my chosen. . . . When you chose Me*
> *You were made Mine. . . .*
> *All you who choose*
> *To bear with me the bitter burden of things . . .*
> *. . . whether you give*
> *Your bodies to be burned, your hearts to be broken,*
> *Or only stand and wait in the marketplace*
> *For work or bread. . . . it is I who stand and suffer with you."*

That same summer of 1946 a young woman who was a lecturer in Italian at Cambridge University was the organizing secretary of a Summer School for the Society for Italian Studies.

Her name was Barbara Reynolds. Her husband, Lewis Thorpe, was recently demobilized from the army and had been appointed Lecturer in French at Nottingham University, where he later became a professor. The Thorpes had a four-year-old son named Adrian.

Barbara Reynolds had seen the announcement put out by Penguin that Dorothy was working on a new translation of Dante. The organizing committee thought that a celebrity like Dorothy would be a great drawing card for their Summer School (and as one of them said, "she could really do no harm"). As secretary Barbara wrote Dorothy to invite her to lecture. She knew almost nothing about Dorothy's work except that she had read *Whose Body?* and heard *The Man Born to Be King.*

Travel abroad was still very difficult, but many people, including the returning students, were eager to get back to their normal studies; so the Summer School session was jammed. The evening of Dorothy's talk, Barbara was very tired and looking forward to sitting down, even possibly to falling asleep with her eyes open, a useful academic trick. The lecture was given in the dining hall of Jesus College, a large medieval hall with oaken rafters and high windows and wainscotted walls hung with portraits. There is a dais at one end with the high table and a minstrel's gallery above the wide door at the other end. The audience sat on backless benches at the long oak refectory tables placed at right angles to the dais where the speakers stood. There was such an overflow crowd that night that chairs were brought in to fill the aisles between the tables.

Dorothy had been dining in Corpus Christi College with a professor of Italian and other university VIPs. She now appeared on the dais with long, dangling earrings, wearing a shimmering silvery gown, which intrigued everyone because during the war nobody dressed up. Her hair was white and short and swept straight back. She wore no makeup, but she looked majestic, and when she spoke in her deep, resonant, faintly amused voice that carried throughout the great hall, Barbara Reynolds was very much impressed. By the time Dorothy had finished speaking, she was fascinated as well.

Dorothy knew that plenty of critics thought that in translating Dante she was over her head. People were already suggesting that she was just a middle-aged popular novelist who was amateurishly dabbling in culture. So in her speech on the Eighth Bolgia in Hell, where Dante and Virgil meet the spirits of Ulysses and Diomedes, Dorothy talked about what a great storyteller Dante was. Everyone recognized that she knew a bit about storytelling.

Barbara Reynolds listened with the conviction that she had finally found someone who saw Dante as real, who could make him come alive as a writer, take him away from the scholars and give him back to the large, popular audience he had written for. She and Dorothy began a correspondence after that lecture which continued until Dorothy's death. They not only met at the many other lectures Dorothy gave on Dante, but they also became close friends. It is obvious from their letters that Dorothy greatly enjoyed having the chance to share her Dante work with Barbara Reynolds, who was fully qualified to judge what she was doing. In fact, Dorothy's growing friendship with the entire Thorpe family was one of the happiest of her later years.

In 1947 Charles Williams, who was still living in Oxford, went into the hospital there and died. His death was a great shock to his friends, many of whom had no idea he was seriously ill. Dorothy had been a friend for many years and part of her joy in translating Dante had come from the fact that Dante meant so much to Williams. He had even told her that he planned to use her letters to him in another book on Dante. When her translation of Dante's *Hell* came out in 1949, Dorothy dedicated it to Williams, "the dead master of the affirmations," quoting from her own translation of the 26th canto of *Purgatory:*

Your verse, forged sweetly link by link
which while our modern use shall last in song,
Must render precious even the very ink.

She and his "Inkling" friends at Oxford had planned to
present Williams with a volume of essays when the Oxford
Press finally moved back to London. Instead, the book, called
Essays Presented to Charles Williams, was his memorial.
Dorothy's contribution described her delight when she first
read Dante. This book with its introduction by C. S. Lewis
helped to give the impression that Dorothy had been a
member of the Inklings too.

Dorothy's translation of *Hell* had been held up by the
national celebration of George Bernard Shaw's ninetieth
birthday and the sudden death of H. G. Wells, both giants in
the English literary world. As she waited for her proof sheets,
Dorothy complained that she and Dante fell between two
stools: she was only fifty and he was over 600 years old, so
neither of them counted for much. She also was sure that
when *Hell* did come out she would be attacked for treating
Dante as a great storyteller instead of as a superhuman "sour-
puss."

She was right. Many reviewers behaved as if she had no
right to translate Dante, and she and Dr. Rieu published an
account of her Oxford education and showed critics copies of
her *Tristan* to prove she was qualified. Some were jealous of
the craftsmanship and speed of her work, others, of her ability
to tell her readers more in her notes and introductions than
they could learn from any other single source. Dorothy was
upset because she knew the fuss was not good for Penguin and
because it was unpleasant to be told she had no right to call
herself a scholar. Her relationship with the press grew even
worse after this, and she often refused to give interviews.

Between 1949 and today more English-speaking readers
have read *The Divine Comedy* than ever before, and most of
them have read Dorothy's translation. Although it is still not

praised by all scholars, it has remained in print and is the most influential and most popular translation on the market. She succeeded best of all with those people she was really working for—the general public. At the same time, her private passion for medieval epics finally became a part of her public image.

In the spring of 1950, when he was sixty-eight, Mac died. Dorothy found his death all the more depressing because at the time she was working dreadfully hard on her Dante and a play for the Colchester Festival. The funeral was held in Colchester, after which the urn containing his ashes was brought back to Witham. Dorothy tried to find time to carry out his wish that his ashes be scattered in Lanarkshire, Scotland, where most of his family was buried. Later that spring, the local doctor was going to Lanarkshire on vacation, and Dorothy asked him if he would take Mac's ashes there for her, which he did. After Mac's death, Dorothy invited friends to visit her and she spent more time in London, sometimes staying with friends like Charis Frankenburg, who had moved south after the war.

It was during 1950 that Dorothy was made an honorary Doctor of Literature by the University of Durham. She bought herself a new fur coat to celebrate, and it was said in Witham that she never took it off again. She was always pleased when people called her, quite correctly, "Dr. Sayers."

The Public Orator who gave the main speech at her installation began by making a number of puns based on her mysteries, suggesting that a gallows would be a more appropriate place for her to stand than a speaker's platform. He went on to say that her novels had given more pleasure to educated readers than any other written since Sherlock Holmes, and that her novels also illustrated society's problems and reflected Dorothy's breadth of outlook and strong moral sense. Finally he said that in conferring upon her a doctorate of letters the university was expressing its admiration for her art, gay or grave, and a deep regard for her sincerity.

Dorothy's longest and most elaborate play, *The Emperor*

Constantine, was produced during July 1951 at Colchester as a part of the Festival of Britain celebrations. She had been working on it for over two years. Dorothy had chosen to dramatize the story of Constantine the Great, who died in 337 A.D., a baptized Christian and sole ruler of the civilized world. It was his adoption of Christianity as the state religion of the empire that changed Christianity, almost overnight, from a persecuted minority to a great earthly power. As Dorothy demonstrated, such a change meant that Christianity had to face two problems it still has not solved—the relationship between church and state, and the relationship between heretic and orthodox.

Constantine himself is a shadowy figure with many contradictions, and Dorothy had to interpret the facts as best she could to produce a reasonable and consistent story. She used not only historical facts but also legends, such as the one that Constantine's mother was a Christian, Helena, the daughter of old King Coel of Colchester.

Constantine not only conquered the entire Roman Empire and made it Christian, but he called the great Council of Nicea at which the theologians of East and West wrote the Nicene Creed, which is still one of the most important creeds for orthodox Christianity. Constantine, therefore, was a challenge worthy of Dorothy's craftsmanship. After two years' hard work she had produced a "chronicle" play (one that lists events in order without interpreting them) which had twenty-five scenes and ninety-four characters. The action ranges all over the Mediterranean world. The scene which has become best known is the third act, in which Dorothy actually stages the Council of Nicea, with the Western bishops pitted against Arias, the Eastern bishop who denied Christ's divinity.

As usual Dorothy took a hand in the production. Among her unpublished papers is a small notebook with a separate page for every member of the cast. The actor's name and address are listed, then his measurements, and the character, or characters, he will play. Dorothy also inspected sets, helped cast the play, and worked on the script at rehearsals, cutting up speeches and reorganizing the many scenes. She not only enlisted the aid of her friend the Witham jeweler, but she also made some of the ornate jewelry herself and is given credit for it in the program. The incredible number of costumes needed were designed by her friend Norah Lambourne and made by the Colchester Centre's Women's Institute. All sorts of people helped get the play together: the Colchester District Commander, Major-General Sir Hugh Stockwell, who loaned soldiers to play parts and stored scenery at his army base; students from the North East Essex School of Art, who painted scenery and made props; the Colchester Centre's Women's Institute, who made the costumes; the landlord of the Red Lion Hotel, who let the cast rehearse in his ballroom; and the many local people who acted in the play.

The first night, the play ran more than four hours, and the audience was exhausted by the amount of history it had lived through. The reviews were mixed. Some critics were bored by what they thought was a dramatized church row; others felt that the costumes, scenery, and set changes overwhelmed the story, or that Constantine remained too shadowy. But most people praised the Council of Nicea scene as great theater. Dorothy took a curtain call opening night, looking like a character herself in her backstage costume of a crumpled white dress and tennis shoes. The play's third act was put on later at her parish church in London.

12

LAST WORKS

In January 1952 Dorothy was elected a church-warden at St. Thomas' Church, Regent's Street, in London. Her job, according to her vicar and old friend the Reverend Pat McLaughlin, was to help prepare for the church services, assign seats to parishioners, and keep order during services. She was even supposed to take offenders in custody if necessary! Women had not been churchwardens in the Church of England before the war, and even now they were uncommon. As an adult Dorothy had refused to do "church work" of the kind thought suitable for women—that is, helping out with the choir or the altar guild or running church bazaars. But the post of churchwarden suited her perfectly, and she began to devote more time to her London parish.

On some occasions she read the Epistle at Communion services, wearing her academic cap and gown. This costume not only was entirely appropriate for church occasions, but it helped to disguise her ever increasing bulk in a majestic fashion. She brought famous people to speak to the Society of St. Anne and stayed about herself, talking late at night to those who were interested. She was warm and friendly and quick to speak up if she felt the discussion was getting over people's heads. After the war St. Thomas' became well known for its productions of religious plays, not only Dorothy's but also of playwrights like Christopher Fry.

Both St. Thomas' and St. Anne's had been so badly damaged by bombs that the church authorities finally decided to tear St. Thomas' down. That parish and St. Anne's, where only the tower was left standing, were combined with St. Peter's, which celebrated its two hundredth birthday in 1952. These combined parishes were then known as the Parish Church of St. Anne's with St. Thomas' and St. Peter's. As Churchwarden Dorothy worked extremely hard, writing letters and appeals, attending innumerable committee meetings, in aid of a project to build a new "multi-media" chapel on the site of St. Anne's nave. It was to combine a movie house, theater, and lecture hall, all in the heart of London, but nothing more was accomplished than to clear St. Anne's of rubble and make a parking lot. The tower, left standing in its old churchyard, has a garden for passersby to sit in.

Dorothy's political views were still strongly Conservative, and as a loyal party member she had attended some of the Queen's Garden Parties. During the General Election in 1950, she had agreed to help out at a Conservative meeting in Witham. Her friend, the rector Aubrey Moody, was the local Tory candidate for Parliament. Dorothy had the job of trying to keep the meeting going until he and another speaker arrived. To do so, she delivered a speech on King John and the *Magna Charta* which the Witham voters, many of them Laborites, did not care for. They had packed the gallery, hoping to break up the meeting, and now they heckled Dorothy, shouting out rude remarks like, "Go back to your books, Momma," and "Pig! Pig!" a reference, it seemed, to the Flemings' pig-keeping, not Dorothy's size. When the candidate arrived, they called him "Audrey." After that Dorothy kept her political activities to occasionally cooking supper for Mr. Moody as he dashed from one meeting to another.

She continued to give many talks, often on Dante, and

to work on her translation of his *Purgatory*, the place where the souls of sinners are reeducated so they are ready to meet God. She felt that *Purgatory*, while the least known, is the most tender and human part of the *Comedy*, giving the reader something quite unlike the appalling fascination of hell or the intellectual severity of heaven.

She and Barbara Reynolds wrote letters back and forth about her translation, and she occasionally went to visit the Thorpe family, which now included a daughter, Kerstin, born in 1949. The Thorpes had the feeling that their way of life reminded Dorothy pleasantly of her early years in Bloomsbury. One time they drove through the Fens and she showed Barbara the old rectory in Bluntisham where she had grown up, commenting on how big and inconvenient it had been. Another time when she came to stay with them and give a speech on teaching Latin, she went the next afternoon to have tea with C. S. Lewis.

Dorothy was still writing her other friends about her work, particularly to Scott-Giles, who drew the illustrations for the Penguin edition of the *Comedy*, including the diagram of the Universal 24 hour clock which shows the time of day in the northern and southern hemispheres.

In November 1953 and January 1954 a new kind of "spoof" article by Dorothy appeared in *Punch*. These "Pantheon Papers" are witty and highly sarcastic attacks on the post-Christian world with its tendency to worship many gods. They are also a parody of the *Book of Common Prayer*.

One group of the papers has a new church calendar to fit the times, called a "Calendar of Unholy and Dead-letter Days." Some of its major feasts are St. Lukewarm the Tolerator, Lowbrow Sunday, All Fools Day, and the Theophany of the Spirit of Progress, commonly known as Petrol Sunday. Its church seasons begin with Advertisement and go through Trash Wednesday to the pestilential season of Umbrage. These *Punch* articles make fun of the institutional church and clergy for giving in to modern, secular culture. They represent

Dorothy at her sharpest "bearding the bishops" or "engaging in her diabolical occupation of going to and fro in the world."

Between 1953 and 1956, in her spare time, Dorothy also wrote out the short texts for a series of Advent calendars for children which were illustrated by Fritz Wegner. The first was called *The Days of Christ's Coming,* and next two were *The Story of Adam and Christ* and *The Story of Noah's Ark.* At the same time, many of her novels and short stories were being broadcast and rebroadcast in various forms on the B.B.C. radio, and during the 1950's on television as well. *Busman's Honeymoon,* which MGM had made into a movie in 1940, was also done on B.B.C. television in 1947 and 1957 and on radio in 1949 and 1965; *The Nine Tailors, Murder Must Advertise,* and *Strong Poison* all were broadcast too.

Dorothy's first book of speeches and articles on Dante was published in 1954. It was called *Introductory Papers on Dante* and was dedicated to the "Organizers and Students of the Summer Schools . . . who so kindly encouraged me to talk to them about Dante." Those organizers included, of course, Barbara Reynolds, who wrote the preface to the book. In this preface Barbara says that Dorothy was giving Dante back to the ordinary reader for whom he wrote. She also reminded the reader that the best place to find Dante is "alive in his writing." This phrase struck Dorothy as a perfect summary of what she felt about literature and its authors. After all, as she wrote to Barbara when she thanked her for the preface, "One can't make up fancy psychology about the unknown author of *The Song of Roland.*"

These days Dorothy had the habit of going by train to London on Tuesdays and coming back to Witham on Friday evenings. She was regularly met by the local taxi driver. She was much better known in Witham now, and many people remember having amusing conversations with her. One was the jeweler who had helped out with the costumes for *Constantine,* who also came to fix her clocks. She loved to hear "Grandfather" clear his throat before he struck the hour, she once remarked, referring to the fact that grandfather clocks give a warning click before they strike.

She was also a familiar figure in the local bookstore and had appeared uninvited at its grand opening (the owners had not dared invite her). She liked to browse about and to chat with anybody in the shop, so long as they did not talk about her. She was very good for business because people came in to listen to her and she bought a lot of books. The shop owners remember that she always bought the newest book by Tolkien as soon as it came out.

Dorothy's translation of *Purgatory* came out in 1955. In her introduction, she talks about how Dante manages to produce surprise and variety in two long poems which have almost the same subject. For in hell and purgatory the punishments are not very different—the difference is in the attitude of the sinners. In either you get what you want. If you want your own way forever, you can get it in hell; if you want God's will, you get it by going through purgatory. In *Purgatory* Dante's writing becomes the "very stuff of fairy-tale . . . and of all the romances . . . [with] its sparkle and gaiety and its reunion of true lovers after . . . separation." Purgatory also is not eternal, but exists in time.

Critical comments about *Purgatory* were less strident than they had been for *Hell*, but many reviewers still opposed Dorothy's using Dante's three-line stanzas, while others complained that she was not only lecturing them on Christian theology but insisting that Dante was a comic writer. But the general reading public bought her translation of this book as enthusiastically as they had the first and sent her fan letters about how much they enjoyed it. Teachers wrote her that she had helped get their students to read and like a classic.

One new reader especially delighted Dorothy. In September 1956 Barbara Reynolds and her son Adrian, who was fourteen, were at home alone and she suggested that they read Dorothy's *Hell* aloud. Once started, they read straight through it in three days. When Dorothy heard of their feat, she wrote back awarding Adrian "First Prize for staying power in the form of a Collar of the Ancient Order of the Bulldog, First Class with Studs." She offered his mother a silver clarion and a bottle of throat lozenges. "That," she told them, "is the way to read Dante!"

Before she began to tackle *Paradise* (or *Heaven*), Dorothy took time out to do another project for Penguin which she had been wanting to do since her college days. She made a new translation of the *Song of Roland,* the medieval French epic about Emperor Charlemagne's legendary nephew Roland. Dorothy had always been stirred by the heroic in literature and life, and a poem like this one, with a long historical tradition, meant a lot to her. She was also moved to tackle the translation right then and there because her old Oxford tutor Mildred Pope was deathly ill. Sadly enough, Miss Pope did not live to see the finished translation. She was a friend of the Thorpes also, and Dorothy told them that she expected Mildred Pope in heaven to inhabit Dante's fourth Heaven of the Sun, where the great angelic doctors and teachers lived. Both the Thorpes helped Dorothy with *Roland,* and her friend Norah Lambourne drew the illustrations of Norman costume and armour.

Dorothy made her translation as close as she could to the original ten-line French stanzas with their use of assonance, or similar-sounding syllables, instead of rhymes. She recommended getting a feel for how the poem would have sounded chanted aloud in a medieval hall by reciting it in the bathroom where there are many hard surfaces to reflect the sound in the proper way. Her friend Val Gielgud reported that he had been astonished and excited by the sound of the poem in French when Dorothy declaimed a few lines for him. She told him that by comparison modern French is very thin-sounding.

Unlike Dante's universe, the world of Roland is young, a place where loyalties and actions are simple to understand. Like a play, the epic has very little description and brief stage directions. Its characters are both real and fairytale. Some, like Charlemagne, are shown as older and larger than life, but very human too, riding among his barons as the greatest baron of them all. Even the pagans are noble fellows who are wrong because they worship false gods. The poem is Christian—unlike *Beowulf*, for example—but it is a simple, uncomplicated Christianity. The Christian warriors who die fighting for the faith and the king are doing their duty, and they will lie on beds of flowers in Paradise.

Roland's battle scenes, however, are long and graphic. The people for whom the poem was written were interested in technique and strategy, just as if the heroes were playing cricket or baseball. They wanted to hear a little about the main players.

> *The County Roland throughout the field goes riding;*
> *With Durendal, good sword, he stabs and slices,*
> *The toll he takes of Saracens is frightful.*
> *Would you had seen him, dead man on dead man piling,*
> *Seen the bright blood about his pathway lying!*

Oliver, Roland's dear friend and companion, is the traditional friend of the hero—blunt, hard-headed, and loyal. He sees how many Saracens there are and urges Roland to sound his horn for Charlemagne to come to the rescue; and although he fights grimly before dying, he also tells Roland bluntly,

> *"Companion, you got us in this mess.*
> *There is wise valor, and there is recklessness...*
> *Ne'er shall we do service to Charles again...*
> *Your prowess, Roland, is a curse upon our heads."*

Here, just as Dorothy said, are Lord Peter and Charles Parker in another age.

About the time that *Roland* was published in 1957, Dorothy's *Further Papers on Dante* also appeared. Dorothy was continuing to give lectures and was at work on the *Paradiso*. She had finished about the first twenty cantos (out of thirty-three) when, on December 13, she went to visit the Thorpes in Cambridge. While she was there, she read Barbara her translation of the twentieth canto and talked about the problems of the translation, adding that the thought of doing the notes for this volume made her feel quite faint. Saturday morning, December 14, the two of them went to the Fitzwilliam Museum to see an exhibition of the paintings of the poet William Blake. Dorothy then insisted on walking about Cambridge in search of a recording of Beethoven's Fifth Symphony for Adrian Thorpe's Christmas present. Dorothy plodded along very slowly because of her weight. They had lunch at the Blue Boar on Trinity Street, then her car arrived to drive her back to Witham, and the Thorpes never saw her again.

Back home that weekend, Dorothy had her old friend Val Gielgud to tea. He had come to interview her for *The Sunday Dispatch,* and in his article he commented that she had seemed to be her usual, brisk, amusing self, full of plans for the future. She was impatient with her public's demand for more Lord Peter stories and insisted that her real talent lay in her translations. Lord Peter was only her "bread-winner." That same weekend the Witham's butcher's cat was run over, and Dorothy came into the store to tell him how very sorry she was to hear the sad news.

On Tuesday, December 17, Dorothy went by train to London to finish her Christmas shopping. A friend who caught sight of her that day thought she looked very tired. Dorothy caught the evening train back to Witham, where the taxi driver, Mr. Lapwood, met her at the station and drove her home.

What happened after that reminds one of her own mystery stories. Wednesday morning her gardener-handyman arrived to find lights blazing in her bedroom and her precious fur coat and bag dumped on the bed. She herself was crumpled up, dead, at the foot of the stairs, and the cats had not been fed.

A postmortem was held in Chelmsford, where it was diagnosed that she had died of heart failure. Her death may have been brought on by her excessive weight and smoking, but also, perhaps, by the fact that she had lived an extremely active life, with many stresses and strains. She was sixty-four years old.

The first person the Witham people called was Muriel Byrne. She came at once to take charge and was the one who found Dorothy's will, made some twenty years earlier, lying hidden in a dresser drawer. Dorothy's death was noted in newspapers around the world. Her obituary in the Witham paper said that she was a familiar figure in the town and had brought much fame to the area. As she requested in her will, in which she named Muriel Byrne as her literary executor and made her son Anthony her sole heir, her body was cremated at Golders Green, and her ashes placed under the floor of the tower of St. Anne's, Soho. A plaque was dedicated there in June 1978.

There was a formal Memorial Service for her at 12:30 p.m. on January 15, 1958, at St. Margaret's Church, Westminster. This is the gothic "Parliamentary" church next door to Westminster Abbey. The Archbishop of Canterbury was represented by the Reverend Eric Jay, and Canon Michael Stancliffe officiated at the service, assisted by her old friend and vicar Pat McLaughlin. The "Red" Dean of Canterbury was there representing the Cathedral, and six bishops of the Church of England: the bishops of Peterborough, Lichfield, Chelmsford, Kensington, and Colchester, as well as her old friend Bishop Bell of Chichester. Bishop Bell read a panegyric which had been written for the occasion by C. S. Lewis, who had once said that Dorothy had the same appeal for him as a bracing high wind, an apt description of the coming of the Holy Ghost at Pentecost.

The First Lesson from the Book of Wisdom was read by Val Gielgud, and the Second Lesson from Revelation by Judge Gordon Clarke. Together with her son and her old friends, there were lords and ladies, official representatives of universities, writers and scholarly organizations, drama groups, parish councils, and publishing companies. The service ended with Abelard's hymn, "O Quanta Qualia," which Dorothy had sung long ago at Oxford in the Bach Choir:

O What their joy and their glory must be
Those endless Sabbaths the blessed ones see;
Crown for the valiant, to weary ones rest:
God shall be all, and in all ever blest.

At the end of the service everyone present was given a miniature copy, bound in white leather and trimmed with gold, of Dorothy's own essay "The Greatest Drama Ever Staged."

In another essay she wrote for the *Sunday Times* in June of the year she died, Dorothy had explained that Christians see this world as a novel, which has a whole universe of action within its pages but no independent reality. Its reality depends on God, who alone is real in His own right. But man is made able to enter this true reality, which is called heaven, so that when he dies, "It is not as though the characters and action of the book were continued in our next like a serial; it is as though they came out from the book to partake of the real existence of their author."

POSTSCRIPT

AFTER HER SUDDEN DEATH, THE FIRST MAJOR PROBLEM
that faced her executors was what to do about the unfinished
translation of Dante's *Paradise*. Muriel Byrne remembered
having a somewhat casual conversation with Dorothy about
being her literary executor, during which she had protested
that she could not handle the Dante. Dorothy had airily replied, "Oh, Barbara will see to that." Consequently, the
executors invited Barbara Reynolds to complete the translation. In an interview with Dr. Rieu at Penguin, Barbara explained that she had never done that kind of verse translation.
He gently but firmly suggested she try.

Barbara Reynolds went home and looked through
Dorothy's notebooks and letters again and discovered that she
had a fairly clear idea of how Dorothy had meant the rest of
the translation to go, along with a few bits and pieces of the
missing parts. She knew various details too, such as why
Dorothy preferred some kinds of rhymes to others. As encour-
agement she had a letter from Dorothy herself, written the
year before when Barbara had returned from a trip to Italy and
had called to say that she was home again. In the letter
Dorothy had told her that she was greatly relieved and delighted to hear her voice. She was expecting Barbara to found
a new school of humane Dante studies, so she must not fall

into the sea or do anything tiresome until she had done her job of carrying the torch.

Many people rallied around to help her. Scott-Giles drew the diagrams and illustrations, while the Dante scholar, Geoffrey Bickersteth, with whom Dorothy had been corresponding, offered to assist in any way he could. The finished translation of *Paradise* came out in 1962. The introduction and notes were written by Barbara, and the difficulty of the whole task was expressed by a quotation from the 30th canto on the frontispiece, a tribute to Dante and to Dorothy also:

> Now in her beauty's wake my song can thrust
> Its following flight no farther; I give o'er
> As, at his art's end, every artist must.

Their combined third volume was also highly successful, and most people do not sense where the "join" comes unless they look it up.

When she was asked if Dorothy had any idea she would not live to finish the *Comedy* translations, Barbara replied that she doubted if Dorothy would have taken time out to do the *Roland* if she had expected to leave Dante undone. Dorothy had also been devoting many hours to the St. Anne's project, using time and energy she did not have to spare.

Paradise is a story about ordinary human beings acquiring a taste for the joys of heaven. Dante grows in grace and understanding as he moves from circling sphere to sphere until at last his will and desire are combined with the Divine Will. Many readers have found *Paradise* hard to understand, but this translation makes the trip as easy as possible. With the help of her friends, Dorothy had done what she set out to do— reintroduce Dante and his ideas to the modern world.

In the time since her death, Dorothy's friend Marjorie Barber has also died, after a long, difficult illness, while Muriel Byrne, at over eighty, is completing her life's work, an edition of the Lisle Letters. These are a collection of letters from a noble family in Tudor times with which she hopes to recover "the lost moment that was Tudor England." When published, these letters, selected and translated by her into modern English, will fill six volumes. Charis Frankenburg, now retired from the Bench, has recently written an autobiography called *Not Old, Madam, Vintage,* and Scott-Giles has published his Wimsey Family history, made up of the long spoofing correspondence he and Dorothy carried on about the Wimseys.

Several collections of Dorothy's writings have been published in the past twenty years, edited in different ways, but all aiming to show that she was a consistent writer and thinker. A group of her essays called *The Poetry of Search and the Poetry of Statement* came out in 1963. In 1969 another collection called *Christian Letters to a Post-Christian World* appeared. Then in 1971 her two essays on women were published as a pamphlet, and a collection of all the Lord Peter stories also came out, including one story never published before about the Wimseys and their children at Talboys. Selections from her works under various headings like "women, work, language and sin" were put out in 1973 under the title *A Matter of Eternity.*

That same year the last three Wimsey stories were published together in England, with an introduction by Janet Hitchman, who had done a show for the B.B.C. on Lord Peter. This introduction included a few facts about Dorothy's life, but Dorothy had never been talkative about her personal life, and partly for fun she had even confused people or misled them. Her abiding conviction was that an author should be found "alive in his work."

Then the B.B.C., at the urging of actor Ian Carmichael, who had long wanted to play the part of Lord Peter, decided to do a whole new series of television shows based on her mysteries. They shot the shows on location, in color, and a whole new generation discovered Dorothy L. Sayers. When these B.B.C. productions were shown in the United States, there was an outburst of interest in Dorothy herself, and a British publisher persuaded Janet Hitchman to collect what facts she could and write a biography. This book appeared in 1975 with the title, *Such A Strange Lady,* a phrase supposedly used by many of the people who had come in contact with Dorothy.

About this time, people in Witham who had been endeavoring to keep her memory alive there persuaded the Essex County Council to honor her by restoring her home as two separate cottages and installing a plaque on them in a public ceremony held on November 15, 1975. Ian Carmichael unveiled the tablet, while the members of the newly formed Dorothy L. Sayers Literary and Historical Society looked on. It says *Dorothy L. Sayers, 1893–1957, novelist, theologian, and Dante scholar.*

In 1976 Dr. Clyde Kilby of Wheaton College in Wheaton, Illinois, announced that Wheaton's Wade Collection had purchased most of Dorothy's unpublished papers from her estate. (This group did not include most of her letters, which were found molding in the attics at Witham and which Muriel Byrne persuaded Anthony Fleming to scrape up and keep.) The Wade Collection had been founded to preserve the works of seven important Christian writers: C. S. Lewis, Charles Williams, Owen Barfield, J. R. R. Tolkien, George MacDonald, G. K. Chesterton—and Dorothy herself.

But perhaps the most fitting tribute to Dorothy's life is a memorial on a wall of the chapel at Somerville College. It reads:

In Memoriam
Dorothy Leigh Sayers
Scholar of Somerville College
M. A. Oxon. Hon. D. Litt. Durham
Born 1893 Died 1957
"Praise Him that He hath made man in His own image,
a maker and craftsman like Himself."

Key to Map Numbers

1 Oxford

2 London

3 Witham

4 Colchester

5 Salisbury

6 Canterbury

7 Kirkcudbright

8 Hull

9 Lichfield

10 Cambridge

11 The Fens (Ely)

IRIS
SE.

ATLANTIC
OCEAN

V